Silence Shattered

An Eyewitness Account of the Columbine Tragedy

Heidi Johnson

insight publishing group

Tulsa, Oklahoma

Silence Shattered

Silence Shattered by Heidi Johnson
Published by Insight Publishing Group
8801 S. Yale, Suite 410
Tulsa, OK 74137
918-493-1718

Scripture quotatoins marked KJIV are taken from the New King James version of the Bible. Copyright ©1979, 1980, 1982, 1994 by Thomas Nelson, Inc., publishers. All other scripture quotations are taken from the New International Version. Copyright © 1973, 1978, 1984 by International Bible Society. Used by permission of Zondervan Publishing House. All rights reserved.

Cover design by Jeffrey Mobley

ISBN 1-930027-43-5
Library of Congress catalog card number: 2001094072

Printed in the United States of America

DEDICATION

I dedicate this book to my dad, who never gave up on me. Thank you for encouraging me and being the godly example that has brought me this far. I look forward to seeing you in heaven.

Contents

Foreward

Looking back on my life—especially the past three years—I see the changes and trials that have sculpted me into the person that I am today. Certain events have been significant in the formation of my mental and spiritual fabric. Although I have had to endure a lot, one thing has remained the same—Christ's love. It found me when I was alone on my bed with no friends as easily as it found me hiding under a table with gunfire over my head. Even when I went astray, Jesus Christ's love was the first thing to reach out to find me.

By reading this, I hope you gain more than just a story. I would be glad if you were inspired, yet I would be thrilled if that inspiration led you to change. If anything, my hope and prayer is to bring the lost to Jesus Christ and to motivate Christians to a new level of intimacy in their walk with God.

Throughout this book, keep in mind that though I am an ordinary teenager, I serve an extraordinary God. I want no credit or recognition from this book; all I want is to make Christ known so that He may have the glory. If no one is changed through my writing, my work is in vain. Therefore, my goal is only to honor Christ and His desire to reach the lost. Thank you for reading.

Part I
My life

As I crouched under my table, the prank became a reality. Bombs went off right outside the library while smoke filtered into the room and screams filled the air. Chills ran down my spine, and my heart sank into my stomach.

"Lord, I thank You for Your protection," I prayed. "I thank You that You will never leave me nor forsake me. I thank You for Your peace."

My prayers were soon interrupted by the two black shadows that entered the library, emerging through the smoke. A short boy wearing army fatigues and a white shirt with red letters on it walked in first, and following him was another one, dressed in black from his head to his toes and wrapped in a gothic trench coat. They had ammunition strapped to their shoulders and machine guns in their hands. Both of them grinned as they said, "Everyone in this library, get ready to die!"

I heard shouts as they fired the first deafening shots. "Everyone get ready to die!" they shouted again. Evil filled the air, but even then Jesus stayed close to me.

Chapter One

THE DOWNWARD SPIRAL

I never did anything wrong in elementary school and was always the goody-goody. I never thought about smoking or drinking or rebelling. Probably the worst thing I ever did my whole elementary career was lie, and even then I felt so bad afterward I had to confess. I would even apologize for doing things that weren't wrong such as taking a paper clip from my teacher or asking a friend for help on my homework. My actions reflected a state of paranoia in which I was afraid to do anything wrong. Feelings of inadequacy and unimportance robbed me of my joy, and although I was not depressed, I was overwhelmed. Before long, high school was around the corner and with it new challenges.

From first to eighth grade, I attended a Christian school that sheltered me from the real world. I am not saying that Christian schools are bad; in fact, I think most kids do not need to be exposed to the world until they are ready and mature enough to handle it. Although my family and I took my maturity into consideration, we decided that going to a public school could be a positive change. My freshman year, I started high school at Columbine High in Littleton, Colorado.

I was filled with anticipation throughout the summer before classes began. The only view I had of public school was through eyes of my friends that went there. My friend Mary seemed to know the ropes of going to a public school, and her brother Allan was going to be a senior the year we started. Although having a buddy who was well prepared for the challenge should have helped, it actually did little to calm my nerves.

I lay awake in my bed for hours the night before the first day of school. Although it was late, I was still wide-awake. The soothing tone of the clock helped, but frightening images flooded my mind. I heaped my covers in a pile at the end of my bed as I tried desperately to get some sleep. I finally managed to get in a few hours, but it seemed that the second I shut my eyes I was awakened by the obnoxious buzz of my alarm clock. I had to get up and get ready.

I nervously ran throughout the house, going about the usual morning routine of a teenaged girl. I was so occupied that I had little time to think about the coming school day. I was a few hundred yards away from the school, riding in our large, old Suburban when it dawned on me. *This is my first day of high school,* I thought. Immediately following that thought, a lump the size of a tennis ball formed in my stomach. I tried to keep calm. "Lord help me, I'm so scared," I silently prayed. *What if the kids didn't like me? What if all my teachers hate me? What if…?* My thoughts were interrupted as my mom pulled up to the curb of the school. She said what moms say, and I was off—out on my own.

My stomach was doing flips as I made my way towards the school entrance. I tried to walk as slowly as possible toward the doors, hoping to prevent the inevitable. In a school of two thousand, I only knew two people and a few acquaintances. One of the two I knew was my best friend, Mary, and the other was her cousin Michelle. My hopes of finding them died when I arrived at the entrance to school. I felt like a small minnow swimming in a big ocean. Unknown faces chattered happily within tiny forbidden crowds of people. I circled the little huddles of teenagers, hoping to spot someone I knew. Panic gripped me as I failed to find even a single familiar face. I had ten minutes until the bell rang, but I really didn't know where to go. I felt like crying on the inside as a voice inside of me screamed, *I hate public school!* My face was red with terror as people giggled loudly within the shelter of their cliques. I was an outsider.

Just as I thought I was going to lose it, I saw a familiar face. Melissa, a girl I had recently met at the movies, came over and offered to hang out with me. Relieved, I walked around with her as she introduced me to all her friends. My hatred of public school diminished, and I began to think more clearly.

Soon the bell rang, and the halls began to fill with frantic teenagers. Books and backpacks and bodies flew through the area as a few hundred kids crammed down a tiny hallway. I said my farewells to my new friends and headed for my first class.

Going from class to class wasn't so bad—at least not as bad as I had envisioned. High school's threats still surrounded me. Fortunately, I actually recognized someone in every class I had!

When lunch arrived, I had the seemingly impossible task of finding Mary. I waited for what seemed about ten years as an endless stream of people passed. I glanced around at everyone in the lunchroom, seeing people of all shapes and sizes, but there was not a whole lot of intermingling in the lunchroom. Everyone was in his or her comfort zone, and talking to me was a step out of that zone. As my panic began rising again, I recognized my friend's familiar face in the crowd. I was saved!

The rest of that week followed the same routine. I spent my days trying to fit in and find my place at my new school. Because Mary's brother was a senior that year, we had the privilege of going out to eat for lunch. That made my freshman life a little more interesting.

> DAY AFTER DAY PASSED AND MY MAIN GOAL BACAME BEING POPULAR.

Day after day passed and my main goal became being popular. As I watched the popular kids from afar, they seemed to have everything together—they dressed well, walked with confidence, and talked to one another as though they had it all figured out—I was just some awkward new kid. Eventually I began making new friends, and although it was hard, I was very determined.

I was determined to be popular.

As time wore on, I developed a bad attitude. Only certain people were "allowed" to talk to me. I placed myself in a specific social class, and only certain classes could talk to other classes. So began my quest for popularity. My priorities began to change and so did my life as I began to find my identity in being popular.

One night my friends and I decided to go to one of the varsity football games. We stood on the crowded stands and watched the game in the cold October weather. We yelled with the crowd as Columbine scored several times against our opponent, Chattfield. Victory seemed inevitable, and sure enough, we won the game. We decided to have a victory dinner at Pizza Hut along with Mary's brother and one of his friends. Time rolled on as we continued our nonsense chatter. I hadn't paid attention to the time, and when I finally did I decided that I needed to call my mom. The time was now 10:30—way past my curfew—and my mother was understandably mad. I reassured her I would be home soon, and with that I hung up.

After reuniting with my friends, we decided to complete our celebration by smoking some cigars. A feeling of uneasiness raced through me, but I did not want to be the party pooper, so I suppressed it. I put the cigar butt to my lips and sucked. It tasted terrible, but I smiled politely and tried to look cool. A few puffs later, we were out of it. Our hysterical laughs echoed throughout the vacant Pizza Hut parking lot. We all piled back into the tiny Honda Civic, and Mary's brother drove us back to our respective homes. As we neared my house, I conjured up a lie to tell my mom in order to cover my sin. My clothes reeked with the stench of cigar smoke, so lying would not be an easy task. Inner guilt continued to rise within my soul, but I kept pushing it down. I felt "good" because I had done a cool thing.

I walked up to the back porch where my mom waited to greet me. One look at her eyes said it all—she knew something was wrong. "Why do you smell like smoke?" She asked.

My level of nervousness rose as suddenly smoking was not so cool anymore. My mom always thought highly of me and trusted me. I knew that my sinful deed would betray her trust. Quickly I began searching the back of my brain for a valid lie. Finally I managed to utter the words, "We were sitting right next to people who were smoking in the stands."

"Then why can I smell it on your breath?" she asked.

"I don't know what you are talking about."

We argued back and forth awhile until she finally let me go to sleep. Before I was dismissed, however, she left me with the piecing words, "Your sin will find you out"—a lesson I would learn several times down the road.

I started drinking—not a lot; it started in little doses. The first time I tasted alcohol was at the church. It was not wine during communion as they do in Catholic churches. It was hard liquor that was not meant to be drunk. I know what you're thinking-how could anyone drink at church?—but keep in mind that I was not living the Christian life.

It happened after the service on a Wednesday night. I went up to the youth room along with my friends. A space that the church loaned out to a private school was connected directly to our youth room. A boy in our youth group smiled mischievously as he proclaimed, "Hey guys, want to see something?"

Mary, Elise, (a girl who went to my church) and I giggled as we curiously followed him into the storage space. He squatted down and pulled up one of the floorboards. "Look what I found!" We sat and stared at the large bottle of peach schnapps. I watched as all my friends took large gulps of the poison, knowing my turn was approaching. Peer pressure weighed heavily on me as I put the bottle to my lips, not knowing what to expect. I took a gulp and tried to swallow quickly. As the liquid hit my taste buds, I tried to force a smile, but the liquor tasted terrible. After I was done, the liquor was placed back in the "vault." We planned to exhume it for further partying in the future.

Although I only had one shot that night, soon one shot became many. I had another encounter with alcohol while I was flying back from summer camp in Texas with my youth group. As the stewardess came by to offer us drinks, one of the boys managed to swipe a can of beer. Since I was in the same row as he was, we decided to split the can. I had ginger ale, so the pale brown color of beer blended nicely with my soft drink. Although it was just a little taste of beer, it brought more compromises to my life, causing me to fall deeper into sin. I didn't understand the power that my new explorations had gotten on my life.

Besides dealing with my friends and the new temptations that seemed to go with them, my family was now facing new challenges. My father had Lymphoma, and my role as the eldest sister widened to include being my sisters' third parent throughout that time. My family endured great adversity, and I admire my parents for being willing to fight. People were constantly over at our house praying for my dad. We never heard the doctor's dismal reports because my dad chose not to believe them. Because of such faith, I can stand today.

Life was incredibly hard during this point. My parents were constantly gone, due to doctor's appointments and treatment, while my friends were always urging me to do things that deep down I knew were wrong.

> I COULD HEAR AN INNER VOICE CALLING ME, "HEIDI, COME BACK."

Every time I sinned, I could hear an inner voice calling me.

"Heidi, come back; Heidi, come back."

"I can't, God. I'm trapped," I'd answer.

"Then let Me free you."

"I can't—I'm too scared." Wrestling with my thoughts, I tried desperately to rid myself of this conviction.

Eventually it left. And that was my downfall.

Chapter Two

PARTY GIRL

Things began looking up the summer before my sophomore year. My dad was feeling better, and I was making more friends. Mary, Elise, and I were labeled as the "Trio". We could not be separated. Every time we got together, we were in our own world—especially Mary and me. We would do the stupidest things and have fun doing them. Making up nonsense words, singing gibberish songs, and goofing off were what we did best. We goofed off so well that we got in trouble on many occasions. After several talks with our youth pastor, being confronted in front of the entire church congregation, and being yelled at on multiple other occasions, we were still as mischievous as ever.

Needless to say, we had quite an impact on our church. No one would sit next to us because we were such a disruption, but it didn't bother us. Every day was a new opportunity to goof off, and I found myself sinking lower and lower. What started as talking in church soon turned into drinking and smoking.

As a sophomore in high school, I began to settle down a little bit. I no longer had the tortures of being a freshman, and more people began to recognize me. School was not as intimidating as it once was. The one disappointment was the fact that Mary and Elise had a different lunch period than I did. I know this might sound silly, but lunch was when all social activity took place. Who you sat with at lunch was who you were friends with for the rest of the year. Your seat in the lunchroom determined your social status. I had other friends to talk to at lunch, but it wasn't the same. I wanted to be with my best friends.

I slowly became more distant from my friends. Several times they promised to call if they chose to go out. I would sit by the phone all night trying to hold back the tears, but many times they failed to call and broke their promises. Finally fed up with the way things were going with my friends, I decided to no longer be a pushover. I sat at my desk and began pouring out my heart on paper:

You said we were friends and friends call each other. I get the impression that you don't want to be with me when you don't call. I am not asking much, but if you don't want to do something with me then let me know. . . .

I continued on for a few more pages and signed, "Sincerely, Heidi." Quietly, I gave them the note the following day at a church service. Mary read it and responded, "Heidi, we love you, and we don't intend to treat you that way." I bought her apology, and things went back to normal; they started calling me more. Thrilled that I was finally getting invited, my parents let me go out; every time I sat home alone it broke my parents' hearts as much as it did mine. Those outings, however, were not in my best interest. I fell into a partying lifestyle. Alcohol had a terrible affect on me, and it caused me to go crazy. It gave me guts. I became popular with the boys (not for good reasons) and began earning a bad reputation at school.

People confronted me and told me that I had changed. Although I knew this was true, I ignored the fact. I didn't care about school, which was obvious because my grades were dropping since I was ditching classes. I didn't care about my family, which was also evident because of all the lies I told, and I especially didn't care about God—I didn't want to be robbed of my fun. This was my life, and I wanted to live it the way I wanted to. No one could tell me otherwise.

My parents had several chats with me about my behavior. As they talked, I would put my brain on autopilot, nod my head, and allow what they said to go in one ear and out the other. Oftentimes my mom would bring up issues about God. I would get angry because I didn't want to be bothered. *You can't tell me what to do,* I would think silently.

Not only was I dishonest with the ones I loved, I was dishonest with myself. I kept telling myself that I liked partying, while inside I was a little girl crying for help. At night I would cry out to God, desperately wanting a way out, but one thing stood in the way of my freedom—my friends. I was too scared to say no, too scared

> AT NIGHT I WOULD CRY OUT TO GOD, DESPARATELY WANTING A WAY OUT.

to get out of my sin, and too scared to look unpopular. All of this changed one night.

It was Mary's birthday party. The impression was that it would be all girls and that there would be parental supervision. After much begging, my parents agreed that I could go. Overjoyed, I shoved twenty dollars into a birthday card and had my dad drop Mary and me off.

"I'll spend the night," I said.

With a look of disapproval my dad replied, "Heidi I want you to call me at twelve."

"Sure, Dad," I replied. And with that I was off to one of the worst nights of my life.

The party was held at a girl named Erin's house. It was held there for two reasons. The first was that her parents wouldn't be home, and the second was that even if her parents had been home, they wouldn't have cared. Mary and I walked into the tiny town home, and I saw three girls sitting at the kitchen table. We said our hellos, and the party started. The counter was filled with several bottles of liquor as well as the usual snack foods such as chips, pretzels, and popcorn. My friends knew how well—or rather, poorly—I held my liquor, and whenever I got drunk they made me promise to be careful. I agreed again this time, and down went the first shot of tequila. From that point on, the entire night was a haze.

I remember busily talking to two other girls at the party. Our conversation was interrupted by a knock on the door. A stripper dressed as a fireman walked in the room and began to do his dance. I only made it through part of the dance before my stomach called me to the bathroom. When I walked out, boys filled the house. Although I was drenched in my own vomit (and the liquor I puked up), I partied with the rest of them. I began to get so out of control that I was no longer conscious of what I was doing.

I went upstairs and into the bedroom, where I told some people I needed to call my dad. I fought for composure as a boy handed me his cell phone. I uttered, "Dad I am spending the night—Don't come get me," knowing I would have to stay in order for the alcohol to wear off.

"Heidi, are you drunk?" he asked.

"No, Dad, I'm spending the night!" I responded.

"No, you are not spending the night," he told me. "I am coming to get you."

"No, you can't!"

"I'll be right there." Click.

When Erin heard of my conversation with my father, she was outraged. "What! Your dad can't come over! Get out of my house! I don't want to get in trouble. Get out of my house before I beat the s__t out of you!"

Although I pleaded with her, nothing helped. Soon the party turned into a fight—a fight against me. People who once told me they loved me were yelling in my face. I cried as they threatened me. *What is going on?* I wondered.

At one point I was on my knees begging for mercy. They pulled my hair and smashed my head against the floor. And these were supposed to be my friends? My memory of that night is vague, but before it got any more out of hand, a girl grabbed me and brought me home. I ran inside crying. My parents fired off question after question. I related everything that happened that night. It was the first time I had been truly honest.

My dad looked at me sternly. "You are no longer allowed to be friends with Mary and Elise," he told me.

"Why?"

"Heidi, they are not your real friends," he replied.

And that was it. Everything was through; my world fell—and continued to fall apart for the next couple of days.

I didn't go to school for several days after the party, and when I finally went, I was harassed. One girl, who hadn't been at the party but was part of the inner circle, called me several times. Finally I picked up the phone to see what she wanted. She started by asking for help on English but then started asking me questions about the party. She made me think that she was someone I could trust, and I told her everything. I told her that I had told my parents.

When I finally got back to school, without thinking about it, I went down to the lunchroom as I normally did and sat with my friends. They began talking about me and giving me dirty looks. Someone said, "Hey I know this one girl who went to a party, got drunk, and then told her parents about it!" Laughs erupted from several girls. I forced a smile only to be greeted by stares.

I glanced at Mary, who only stared at me coldly. Erin got up from where she was sitting and screamed, "Why are you sitting here? What are you doing? If I lose one friend over you, I will kill you. Now go! You're not allowed to sit at our table!" Then she pushed me from the table. I got up and glanced around a few seconds more at those I once knew as my friends. *Won't someone speak for me? Won't someone stand up for me?* I wondered. Silence. Nothing but the heartless stares of my friends—my former friends. Unable to breathe, I ran up the stairs while tears began to trickle down my face. I called my dad and had him pick me up.

A line of endless meetings followed that day was—with the police, with my school counselor, with Mary's and Elise's parents. I stayed in the library during lunch hour because I had no friends. I had been deserted.

Every day that I went to school during those remaining months was a challenge. I faced rejection in every classroom I had entered as rumors flooded the school about my infamous night. People were seen as outcasts if they even talked to me. I was untouchable.

There were some benevolent people who still talked to me, one being Rachel Scott, who kindly said I could sit with her and her friends at lunch. Although her offer was much appreciated, I decided to stay in the library. The quiet allowed me to think—something I hadn't thought in a long time.

God began to work on my heart in the stillness that the library provided. Although I was not ready to surrender my life to Him, but He knew it was just a matter of time before I would. With no friends, I had a great deal of free time. I could now spend more time with my family and schoolwork than before. Slowly my grades started improving. Luckily, the incident happened before my grades were able to take a permanent dive. I began developing goals for a career and began working to pursue those goals.

Working one night on a project, I had to use the Internet for research. I logged on and noticed that I had a new e-mail. As I pulled it up, I realized it was from Mary. She entitled the letter "Three Friends" and then graphically depicted what happened at the party. After the story, it went on to say how we would never be friends again and that if I so much as even told anyone about the e-mail, I would really have problems.

As I read the conclusion of the letter, I got an instant message from Mary. "So your on, eh? Well, you probably read the e-mail I sent you."

I sat nervously in my chair as I typed a message back to her. We argued for a while. With every word that was typed, another knife pierced my heart. I was too shocked to cry. Finally, after an hour, she ended by typing simply, "I'll never talk to you again." Crying, I ran up to

> WITH EVERY WORD TYPED, ANOTHER KNIFE PIERCED MY HEART.

my room. I slammed the door, and the tears I had been bottling up began to flow down my cheeks. *I hate my life,* I thought. *Why am I here? I've lost everything. Nothing matters.* Chills ran up and down my spine, and I felt as though cold blades were piercing my heart. I wanted to die; life was too hard.

Then through the wind came a quiet inward whisper, "I'm still here."

I knew it was Jesus, but why would He want to talk to me? I was a sinner. I had run away from Him.

"It doesn't matter, Heidi, I love you anyway. My blood covers that."

A warm feeling crept over my whole body. I quit caring what other people thought of me. For the first time in two long years, I was free. I felt great! I felt like jumping up, dancing and shouting and praising God. In that moment, in the still-

> FOR THE FIRST TIME IN MY LIFE I EXPERIENCED TRUE LOVE.

ness of the night, I rededicated my heart to Jesus Christ. The prodigal son—daughter—had come home!

For the first time in my life I experienced true love. If anyone had the right to reject me, it was God. But instead He accepted me with open arms. I was lost in my sin, and Christ Jesus found me! He left all ninety-nine sheep to seek just one that was lost. That night I found a treasure more precious to me than diamonds or gold. I found Jesus, and He changed my life around completely. I no longer had the desire to do the things I once did. Even the thought of alcohol disgusted me. I was free!

I was now in the light that removed the chill of the darkness. I was finally who I wanted to be, and it was all thanks to Jesus. Some nights I would sit up in my room and think about His love. That He died for me while I was a sinner and hated him overwhelmed me. I finally found what I was looking for. What alcohol could not provide or my friends could not satisfy, He filled. I was a new creation.

Chapter Three

COLUMBINE CROSSFIRE

I looked forward to my times in the library because it was my intimate time with God. During the half-hour, I would pray on paper or write poetry. Christ was so close to me, I could feel Him, and with every written word I expressed nothing but gratitude.

After my rededication, life was good. Looking back, I can see God's hand and His perfect timing in everything. Our church hired a new youth pastor, and what he had to say was exactly what I needed to here. God was doing wonderful things in my life. I loved nothing more than to step into His presence and worship Him. He became my new best friend.

It was now April, and spring was in the air. New evidence of life was all around. Students anxiously awaited the coming break. Although most students started slacking during this time, I began working harder than ever. My goal was to have straight A's, something I hadn't accomplished since the fourth grade.

Although I was doing great spiritually, I had decided to go back to a private school, Faith Christian Academy, the following year. Faith as we call it for short was having cheerleading clinics, and I thought it would be fun to try out. One Monday night, my mom drove me out to the practice. After the clinic I went home and practiced for hours, reciting the same chant over and over again. In a Christian school, performance counts—but so does morality. The following day I would have to pass out forms to several teachers in which they would rate my character. This made me nervous, so as I got ready the following morning I silently prayed, *Lord give me favor.* I prayed this several times that morning. I hoped my teachers would see the change inside of me.

It was April 20, a gorgeous day. The leaves were forming on the trees, and birds sang merrily in the skies. I went to my first four morning classes as usual. I had an algebra test during fourth hour that I was stressed about, but other than that everything was good. God was good.

I went to the library as I usually did for lunchtime. The Columbine library is ingeniously set up with the front overlooking the Rocky Mountains. I could not pass up a chance to enjoy the view, so I found myself a seat near the entrance of the library.

Since I was pressed for time to get homework done, I immediately started doing it. A few minutes into the period, I suddenly heard loud bangs erupting from the back end of the school, close to the library. Remaining completely calm, I told myself it was construction work and continued my homework.

Shortly after that a teacher came running into the room. Her face was pale and she was screaming.

"A kid has been shot! A kid has been shot! Everyone, get under your tables!"

She shouted continuously until she disappeared behind the front desk, where she called the police. *What do you mean that a kid has been shot?* I thought as I got under my table. *That can't be. It's probably all a prank.*

As I crouched under my table, the prank became a reality. Bombs went off right outside the library while smoke filtered into the room and screams filled the air. Chills ran down my spine, and my heart sank into my stomach.

"Lord, I thank You for Your protection," I prayed. "I thank You that You will never leave me nor forsake me. I thank You for Your peace."

My prayers were soon interrupted by the two black shadows that entered the library, emerging through the smoke. A short boy wearing army fatigues and a white shirt with red letters on it walked in first, and following him was another one, dressed in black from his head to his toes and wrapped in a gothic trench coat. They had ammunition strapped to their shoulders and machine guns in their hands. Both of them grinned as they said, "Everyone in this library, get ready to die!"

I heard shouts as they fired the first deafening shots. "Everyone get ready to die!" they shouted again. Evil filled the air, but even then Jesus stayed close to me.

They began in the first section, and I was in the third. I cringed every time I heard a loud blast from one of their guns, but I kept praying. The gunmen made their way over to my section. I could see their boots through the cracks of my table as they passed by. Empty shells rolled on the ground.

"Everyone get up. If you want to live, get up." No one budged, but they didn't stop. The short one chuckled, "This is the best day of my life." They maneuvered all around my section. The boy that was next to me was shot several times, and I could here him moan as he died. They made their way to the window, where they could see policemen pointing their guns at the school.

Again the shorter one spoke. "Look at the f_____ cops out there," he said.

Oh good, I thought. *The cops will be here any moment.*

One of them held a shotgun to the window and fired. The glass shattered, and jagged pieces bounced around on the floor. I could here him laugh, "Hey Dylan, I shot my nose off!"

"You did? Cool."

"Now I have to load up with more shells." He talked in an eerie voice—quiet and soothing while at the same time violent and mad. "Don't worry, you'll all be dead soon. Hey is that one black f_____ dead yet?"

Computer cubicles were directly in front of my table. They pointed their guns and pull the triggers, firing at point blank range. Later I learned that I was in the deadliest section of the library.

Profanity echoed throughout the once silent library. It seemed as though evil lurked in every corner. I lifted up my head and saw one of the shooters. His eyes were a smoky white—he was driven by a power greater than he knew. I ducked back down, hoping they hadn't seen me.

Near the conclusion of the massacre, they stopped directly in front of my table. Their voices could be heard clearly as they plotted to blow up the library. *Fine, blow up the library,* I thought. *I know where I am going if I die. I just want you out of here.* They set off one of their bombs, but thankfully they didn't succeed in blowing up the library.

> HIS EYES WERE A SMOKY WHITE—HE WAS DRIVEN BY A POWER GREATER THAN HE KNEW.

After they were through, they made their way over to my table and looked underneath. I lay crunched in a tight ball. I don't remember whether or not they said anything to me, but then they left the library.

Even after I realized they were gone, I stayed under my table a few more moments before getting up. Pushing the chairs in front of me out of my way and pulling myself up. I didn't know what to do. I wondered if they would be back soon, and I had no idea what to do. The smoke was settling, and I saw Craig Scott helping a girl who had been shot and was covered in her own blood.

I said, "Would it be a good idea if we left?" They agreed and together we prepared to exit the school. We ran out of the library using an emergency exit that was connected to it. I was so relieved to reach the door, realizing that our lives had been spared. We ran outside toward a police car. My eyes were so focused on reaching the car that I didn't stop to look back for even a second.

Once we were behind the police car, those who were unhurt began comforting the wounded. People had been trickling out of the school for a while, and some of them were badly hurt. I prayed loudly as I laid my hands on the injured teenagers. People gave me strange looks, but I kept praying. I wanted to help, and that was all I knew how to do. Everyone did what they could; boys took off their shirts for bandages, and others used socks as tourniquets to prevent more blood loss. As we waited outside the school, watching the police point their guns toward the entrance, another patrol car pulled around.

"Get the wounded in the car first!" he shouted.

I sat next to a boy who lay in a pool of blood. He looked as though he might already be dead, but I saw that he was still breathing. I told him to get up and that there was a police car that would take him to safety, but he didn't respond. I put my arms under his body and tried to hoist him into the car, but I was too weak and he was too big.

"Somebody help me!" I yelled. Several boys came rushing over to help. I grabbed the legs of the boy, and together we got him into the back of the car.

We waited until the police car could take us to safety, and I sat next to a nervous girl with tears streaming down her cheeks. "I don't know if my sister's okay," she said through tears. "She could be dead!" I put my arm around the girl and together we prayed for her sister. When we were done, she looked up with a faint smile.

"We just have to trust God right now," I told her.

Finally, I was able to get into a police car. Sitting next to me were two boys that had been shot in their legs. Each time the car turned, they groaned in pain. The policeman took us to a neighborhood cul-de-sac. When the police officer stopped, I had to try and get one of the boys who had been shot out of the car. I put his armpit under my head and began dragging him over to a grassy lawn. I couldn't get him far, and eventually two men helped me.

Several wounded students were already on the lawn, staining the ground with their blood. It looked like a war zone. One boy was screaming, "He shot my best friend! He killed my best friend!" A lady ran over and began comforting the sobbing boy. I felt helpless. All I could do was pray and comfort them the best I could.

Periodically, an ambulance would come and pick up the most severely injured teens—usually those whose bodies where mangled by the vicious blasts of a shotgun. Something told me I should cry, but I couldn't. I was too shocked.

I was invited into a home where I could stay until my parents were able to reach me. I tried desperately to get a hold of them, but each time I called I got the annoying buzz of a busy signal. I finally reached my mom at work.

"Heidi, are you okay?" she asked.

"Yes, Mom, I'm fine," I told her.

"You aren't hurt, are you?" she asked me.

"No, Mom. God protected me," I responded.

"Did you see kids die?"

I broke into tears. "Yes, Mom, I did." When she didn't immediately ask more questions, I knew my mom was crying too. "Mom, when will you be able to pick me up?"

"I don't know honey, everything is blocked off. Hang in there, okay?"

A feeling of intense disappointment swept over me. There was no one I wanted to see more than my parents. I agreed to be strong, and after saying "I love you," I hung up.

I sat in a stranger's house for hours, watching the news coverage of my high school. The sound of choppers flying overhead occasionally echoed throughout the house. I stood staring at the television for hours, trying to take everything in. I shook uncontrollably, and constant chills ran down my spine.

The thought that I survived the most gruesome and deadly school shooting in American history did not occur to me.

The news was uncertain, and I didn't know if I had lost anyone I knew. My thoughts brought me back to the friends that had betrayed me. I worried that they might be some of the ones that had died, but the thought that they might not know Jesus was the worst, however. I worried that what happened in the library was happening in several other parts of the school. For a long time, I almost felt guilty because I was safe.

I kept praying.

In all of the commotion, I had forgotten completely about my needs, including the fact that I had to go to the restroom. When I got into the bathroom, I noticed my hands were stained with blood. I quickly washed up as new tears began forming in my eyes—I just wanted to get home to my family.

from left to right: Kathy (Mom), me, Heather, Holly, and Barry (Dad)

After what seemed like an eternity, I got a phone call from my dad. He asked the same questions as my mom had asked, and then I pleaded, "Dad, come get me."

"Heidi, it will be hard."

"But Dad, you have to get to me."

Tears peaked in my eyes as my dad said, "Heidi I don't know how long it will take, but I won't give up."

I waited for another two hours. Finally, I heard a knock on the door.

I ran to the door and opened it up to see my father standing in the doorway. It was a reunion beyond words to see someone I might have never gotten to see again.

Chapter Four

AFTERMATH

After the Columbine tragedy, my life was a whirlwind of activity. Interviews and television shows constantly demanded my time. I appeared on shows such as *Dateline* and *Extra*, and our phone was ringing off the hook with more offers. Being on television was exciting at first. I saw it as a chance to share my faith, but the fact was, reporters didn't want to hear about faith—they wanted to hear more sensational details about Columbine. They would ask my opinion on some issues, and when I would give them my answers—they would look at me in a peculiar fashion that showed their disapproval. I would just shrug and carry on.

Several interviews occurred the day after the shooting, and in one particular one, a reporter was very insensitive. My youth pastor, a girl from church(Lauren), and I went to Clement Park where several students gathered to pray and bring flowers to mourn

an interview in Georgia

their lost friends and loved ones. We went to pass out flyers, inviting teens to come to church with us that evening.

When we arrived at the park, I saw that members of the media swarmed the area like vultures. Several students had already been snagged into the interview trap. We began walking around, and soon journalists were requesting interviews. The first one I did was a live spot on a local station telling the television audience that I was looking for my friend Rachel, from whom I had not yet heard. By the time I was on the air, several other television stations had sent their reporters, who quickly began flooding the area.

They began harassing me. "Miss Johnson, would you do a quick interview?"

"Miss Johnson, will you please tell us about your experience?" "Miss Johnson . . . "

One big-time reporter grabbed me, and I agreed to do the interview. After the other reporters saw that I was taken, they began searching for more prey. We went through the usual routine of stating name and grade, and then it was off to the questions. At first the questions she asked were pretty basic—nothing too hard to handle. I felt that it was good for me personally to be sharing my story. She came upon one question asking me about a boy that was killed next to me. I explained that he was shot several times and that the gunmen had come back to make *sure* he was dead.

"No that wasn't good enough please answer again," she snapped.

Puzzled, I answered again. Again she told me that my answer wasn't good enough; apparently she thought I should add a little more feeling to my response. I looked over at my youth pastor. He was giving me the signal that it was time to go. I nodded and said, "Sorry, I have to go now."

The reporter looked at me angrily and said, "No you can't go! You have to answer the question."

So I gave her my final answer and left. I could not believe her insensitivity, but I feel that she probably did not know how her questions affected me, and so I didn't let it get to me; she probably didn't know Jesus, either.

After we finished passing out our flyers, we went back to our church, which was a headquarters for the aid of hurting people. Televisions were set up in the foyer along with some chairs.

Phone banks had been set up where people could call in for counseling.

I went inside, and my mother greeted me; her eyes were red with tears. She spoke gently. "Heidi, they found Rachel."

My eyes lit up. "Is she okay?"

> I FELT AS THOUGH I HAD LOST THE ONLY FRIEND I HAD—THE ONLY FRIEND THAT HAD BEEN TRUE TO ME.

My mom began to cry harder as she shook her head sadly. "She's gone."

Tears began flowing down my cheeks as my mom held me. I felt as though I had lost the only friend I had—the only friend that had been true to me. Several other people gathered around me and comforted me, but I continued to cry. I had never lost a friend like this before.

The one reassurance in this most recent aspect of the tragedy was that I knew Rachel was with Jesus. Several weeks after the tragedy, I woke suddenly with the burden to pray for Rachel. As I started to pray, a presence filled the air. I tried to open my eyes, but it felt as if they were glued shut. When I finally did manage to open them, I saw that a smoky haze had filled the room, and a gentle peace swept over me. Then from the doorway, two shadows came walking in. I saw the silhouette of Jesus holding Rachel's hand as if He were saying, "You don't need to worry about Rachel. I have her now."

Rachel's funeral was to be held at our church—where many of the funerals were held—and though I was still sad, deep down I was happy because I knew that someday I'd see her again.

Media members were always at our church because it was broadcast live around the world. Because of our church's closeness to the tragedy, other churches sent their support to help us. One particular group known as the Master's Commission had driven all the way from Indiana to minister to our youth group.

Our church later got a call from them requesting two Columbine students to speak at their church.

Although our church was very close to Columbine, few students attended our church. Lauren—who was a freshman—and I were chosen to go. I was excited and immediately began preparing what I would say.

Meanwhile, all students had to return back to school. Because of Columbine's poor condition and the fact that it was still a crime scene, we attended our rival school, Chattfield. They set it up so Chattfield students would have classes from seven to twelve and we would have ours from one to six.

Every day back at school was a battle. The slightest sound would cause my heart to race. Fear often bubbled up from inside me. *God, I'm so scared*, I prayed.

"Heidi, I will never leave you or forsake you," He would answer. *But God, I'm scared!* I would reply silently.

"I did not give you a spirit of fear but of power, love, and a sound mind. I am with you always. I saved you once, I can do it again."

My fear would ebb as I quoted scripture. I began to use the Word of God for what it was intended for—a weapon against the enemy, Satan. Although it was not easy to fight, I had no other option. If I was going to be victorious, I had to fight. There were, however, days

> "THE DEVIL IS A ROARING LION, BUT HE HAS NO TEETH."

when I stayed home because it was too hard to face the challenge of going to school. During the aftermath, however, God was with me every step of the way. He covered me that day, and he continued to cover me in the days after. I never experienced nightmares or flashbacks. The only night I had trouble sleeping was the night of the shooting, and I owe it all to God. He sustained me.

Although it seemed to me that the gates of hell had come crashing down, they were no match for the mighty hand of God!

Attacks came from every corner, but Christ continued to rescue me. He sent people across my path to encourage me.

One of the dear ladies of our church sat down with me one day and said, "The devil is a roaring lion, but he has no teeth." I found that to be true every time I walked into the school. I would quote a verse when I first stepped in the door; I could immediately feel the oppression of the enemy weaken. Although there was still no one at school to comfort me because I had lost all my friends, Jesus was there more than ever. He helped me fight.

Soon it was time to leave for Indiana where we were requested to give an interview. I was a little nervous because I didn't know Lauren that well and I had never spoken in front of thousands of people—but I knew God was faithful.

Upon our arrival at the Indianapolis airport, we were greeted by three of the pastors of the Lafayette Assembly of God church, who later become known to us as the "J Team" because their names were Jeff, Jeff, and Jeremy. There was an immediate connection because we were brothers and sisters in Christ. We conducted several interviews in the airport in preparation for attending the Stop the Violence rally.

We were scheduled to speak in a school's Bible club the following morning. Although I had done several media interviews, this would be the first time I would be speaking in front of a crowd about Columbine. Butterflies jumped around in my stomach as one of the students called us up to speak. We made our way towards the front, not knowing exactly what to talk about or how to start. Lauren told her story first. She had been in the cafeteria when the shooting started and ran out with a mob of frightened teenagers. The cafeteria had been the location of the two propane-tank bombs; if these had gone off it would have killed all of the kids in the library and cafeteria together, totaling around five hundred students.

It was my turn to speak next, and I related in detail what happened at Columbine. We then opened it up for questions and answers. Hands shot up across the room as we tried to pick and choose which students to call upon. I felt like a teacher. The questions went right into the first bell, and all the students had to leave. Thus we concluded our first speech. I think we were both rather proud of the outcome.

The day before the big rally, the J Team gave us a tour of the church. As we walked into the sanctuary, my heart leaped as I suddenly remembered a vision God had given me.

The night of the tragedy I had had trouble sleeping. I wasn't scared but was still in shock. As I lay there trying to sleep, I began to see myself preaching to thousands of teenagers about Jesus. Now here was a stage, and it looked just like the stage in my dream! It was confirmation that this was what God was calling me to do.

Later that night and after the tour, I was reading my Bible as I always did, and God showed me a verse that encourages me to this day. It is Jeremiah 1:4-9:

> The word of the Lord came to me saying, "Before I formed you in the womb I knew you, before you were born I set you apart; I appointed you as a prophet to the nations."
> "Ah, Sovereign Lord," I said,
> "I do not know how to speak; I am only a child." But the Lord said to me, " Do not say, I am only a child. You must go to everyone I send you to and say whatever I command you. Do not be afraid of them, for I am with you and will rescue you," declares the Lord. Then the Lord reached out his hand and touched my mouth and said to me, "Now, I have put my words in your mouth. See, today I appoint you over nations and kingdoms to uproot and tear down, . . . to build and to plant."

After reading that, I was prepared for the challenge that followed the next day.

The church members arrived to pray before the big rally began. I sat in one of the chairs, feeling quite nervous. I still considered myself a "baby" Christian and was by no means a trained intercessor. But I sat and quietly spoke my heart to God.

People began flooding the entrance to the church half an hour before the rally began. Overflow rooms were set up in case the sanctuary could not accommodate the two thousand people expected to be there. Five minutes before the start of the rally, all overflow rooms were full and more accommodations were being made. By the time the music finally began, people sat in the hallways to see the rally. It was the greatest attendance their church had ever had.

At the conclusion of the music and other productions, Pastor Booth got up and introduced us with, "Please welcome Heidi Johnson and Lauren Beyer." As we made our way out of our seats, people began to rise and applaud. Tears dampened the corners of my eyes, and I could see that Lauren was crying too. We made our way up to the front of the stage and sat down on the provided stools. We then began by sharing our Columbine stories and then went on to say what Christ was placing on our hearts. Our message was simple—you are not guaranteed a tomorrow. Today is the day of salvation. If you don't know Jesus Christ as your personal Lord and Savior, we told them, don't wait one more minute!

When we concluded our message, it was time for people attending to act upon our words. One of the pastors got up and gave the altar call, then invited people to come up for prayer if they wanted to receive Jesus Christ as their Lord and Savior. I watched as hundreds of people, young and old, got up from their seats and made their way to the front of the church. Tears flowed and lives were touched—including mine. Although I had come to reach the lives of other people, my life was also being touched, and suddenly everything I had gone through was worth it. The pain of all the agony, tears, and disappointments evaporated as I saw the looks of changed people. This was something I wanted to continue doing.

Chapter Five

FROM SEA TO SHINING SEA

Jeremiah 29:11 says, " 'For I know the plans I have for you,' declares the Lord, 'plans to prosper you and not to harm you, plans to give you a hope and a future.' "

After Indiana, I began speaking across the nation. I have traveled from Oregon to Florida, speaking in various venues and sharing the hope of Jesus Christ. I have had the opportunity to reach people of every class, from teens in the inner-city public schools to interdenominational gatherings of believers. I have had the chance to speak to young and old, rich and poor. Each time is a victory against the devil, making him regret the day he ever walked into Columbine. I have seen thousands saved and rededicated and have heard countless stories of people whose lives where touched. Each time I go out, it is an honor just to be a part of what God is doing.

One of the most moving speaking opportunities I had occurred while I was at a public school. A large young man approached me after my message. A crowd had gathered around me, asking questions and what not. The crowd had parted and I saw this boy towering over everyone else and staring at me.

He said, "I need to talk to you," in a rough voice.

At first I thought that he was a member of the press because of his forcefulness, and so I asked him, "Who are you?"

"My name is Joe," he said.

"Okay, Joe. Who are you with?" I asked.

"I'm with this school."

speaking in a public school

"Oh, you're a student." He nodded his head. I explained to him that I would be more than happy to speak with him after everyone had left.

As the gymnasium cleared out, I looked at Joe and said, "All right, I can speak with you now."

He led me over to the bleachers as we sat down. My youth pastor's wife, Melissa, was with me, so she joined us. I watched him for a few seconds as he figured out what he wanted to say.

Finally he said, "I get picked on a lot at school. I don't have any friends and I don't know how much longer I can take it." He paused, "I've thought about shooting up my school."

Words raced through my mind. What do I tell someone thinking about committing a violent crime? Melissa was there to help me as we told him that Jesus loved him and cared about him. We continued talking to him for a good ten minutes and finally invited him to come to a big rally the following night.

The night of the rally, I was in a separate room preparing what I was going to say. The man who was putting on the rally suddenly burst into my room shouting, "Heidi, come here. I have to show you something—hurry!"

I chased him down through several hallways, all the while wondering what could be so important. He led me out to the vast stadium. People had begun to fill the chairs. He said, "Look on the front row at the man in the yellow shirt."

My eyes scanned the crowd and after a moment, I saw a young man wearing a yellow shirt—it was Joe! Later, after I had finished speaking, he approached me and told me he was going to change his life around. He never did snap, as far as I know. God really did get a hold of him.

In July 1999, my pastor and I were invited to speak in Washington, D.C. At the Capitol, I was able to talk with such leaders as Trent Lott— who was the majority Senate leader at the time—and Denny Hasterd-Speaker of the House of Representatives and third in command of the

speaking with Senator Lott

nation—to encourage posting the Ten Commandments in public forums. I had the seat closest to the senator during the meeting. This brought on the envious looks of about twenty clergy members. I was told that the senator was looking forward to hearing from me. The meeting was very formal—much more formal than any I was use to—and I was granted only a small time slot to speak, so I simply said, "Senator Lott, I encourage you and your efforts in posting the Ten Commandments in public places." He smiled tenderly and gave his thanks. I felt honored, as if I had been invited to be in the presence of kings and I was the one they wanted to see. An event like that could be nothing but God.

A rally was also to be held in the nation's capital and would be the first in the capital in seventy-five years. While we were there, I had the chance to speak in the room where Clinton's impeachment trial, the *Titanic* hearings, and the proceedings on the Watergate scandal were held.

Many other doors have been opened for me to preach where I otherwise would not have had an opportunity. On the anniversary of the Columbine tragedy, I had the opportunity to speak in front of twenty thousand people about the love of Jesus Christ. This was then to be broadcast live around the world on CNN. Because this was to be an event where people of all faiths would gather, I was asked to refrain from saying "Jesus." Seeing the opportunity to witness to millions—if not billions—of people, I felt as though I really couldn't do as they asked. I had a long talk with my parents before the event took place. I decided that I did not want to speak if I could not say the name "Jesus." We concluded that I should say whatever God told me to say.

The day of the anniversary, I spoke at our home church. As soon as my speech ended, my father and I got into his Land Cruiser and drove to where the event was to be held. After some nonoffensive music, my father got up to introduce me.

The Bible says that you will receive power when the Holy Spirit comes upon you. I felt that power as I made my way up to the podium to speak. I looked into the vast crowd, took a deep breath, and "unleashed the freak." Some cheered as I proclaimed the gospel, but others remained silent. After preaching, I bid my farewells and took my seat. Two other students followed me, one of whom was a Mormon.

People applauded as the night's meeting ended. I got up from my seat on the stage and was greeted by a Jewish rabbi. She looked at me coldly, said some harsh words, and we both went on our way. I found it interesting, however, that the rabbi only confronted *me*. When the Mormon boy spoke, he boldly professed his faith; but something I said had obviously offended the rabbi. Respect for her as a person kept me from saying, "I don't apologize for what I said."

I found it strangely encouraging, however, that the right person was offended! Throughout the New Testament, Jesus offended people who all had something in common—a religious spirit. People who cling tightly to their legalistic laws seem to get offended more easily than those who look to God for their direction. I think that they are challenged to change and have a hard time accepting that they might be wrong. No one enjoys being told that they are wrong, especially if something in their heart tells them that what they are hearing is right. As I travel, I have offended people with my testimony. Sometimes the truth is more important than their comfort, however. Although it may "hurt" some people, I have to remain faithful to my calling—to preach the truth. God has given me an awesome opportunity to tell the world the Good News.

On one occasion, I was invited to speak in Columbus, Georgia, in some local public schools. These particular schools have predominately African American students and are known for being among the tougher schools in the area. A sense of nervousness crept over me as I got up in front of the large auditorium. The fact that I was in a public school restricted me from trying to convert the students. The principal, however, allowed me to speak about my faith according to me—meaning I could not preach at the students. I made my way up to the podium and shared my story. Every now and then I would hint about my faith. After I gave a simple speech about choices and violence, I opened it up for questions and answers. Several students raised their hands, and I began giving accounts of April 20.

One girl stood up and asked why I felt that I was spared while others died. I thought for a second before answering, "I believe that God has a purpose for my life, and that purpose is to speak to young people." Suddenly all of the background noise ceased. I looked out into the silence in confusion, but suddenly the students began cheering wildly. A smile stretched across my face, and I desperately wanted to preach right then, but I restrained myself. Fortunately, several other questions regarding my faith were asked.

Sometimes God destroys plans to accomplish His work. I was to speak in Daytona at a YMCA prayer breakfast. I had spoken at a similar gathering in Orlando a short time before. It was expected that this event should be the same—strictly formatted and by the book. I had liberty to speak freely, yet, I had to

teens I met at a rally I spoke at

keep in mind that my audience was mostly religious and legalistic. Several denominations would be attending as well as people who did not know Christ. After sitting through the general routine, I got up and told my story. I proceeded to share what I usually spoke about, which was fine with everyone, but God had other plans.

The Spirit of God came upon me, and I began to pour out my heart to some five hundred strangers. People listened attentively as I described the importance of intimacy with Christ. I went on to discuss how easily people get caught in the web of wealth although everything in this world will pass away. I challenged them to lay down their pursuit of riches and follow Christ—where they would find true reward.

The Holy Spirit was touching me so meaningfully, I couldn't control my emotions and began to cry. As I wiped away the tear that trickled down my cheek, I allowed my dad to finish up. Following our standing ovation, a pastor got up. He proceeded to pray about what was planned but then moved a different direction. He ended up giving an altar call! The whole time I sat in my seat, I could feel the presence of God reassuring me that lives where being touched.

Through similar incidences, I have come to learn that God can do more in one second than I can do in an entire lifetime.

One of the best things about speaking in front of people is being able to see lives as they are touched. I spoke in the Sunday youth service at a local church in Oregon. After my dad talked, we gave an altar call. Several people raised their hands to rededicate their lives to God and to receive salvation.

My dad began saying, "Now I want you to come up to the front, so we can pray with you." Several seconds passed as no one came forward. "Many of you raised your hands; I want to know who will be bold enough to come forward," he continued. By now heads began popping up to see if anyone would go forward. No one got up. From the very back row, a girl stood up and began making her way toward the front. When she arrived at the front of the stage, the silence broke into applause. Soon many other students followed her.

Because we were pressed for time, I never had a chance to meet that girl, but later our church received an e-mail relating her story and gratitude. Apparently she was not living her life for God yet desperately wanted Christ to do more in her life. The stand she made that day was the beginning of a life change for her, and I was honored to be a part of it.

Speaking in front of people is not always serious, however. My good friend Lauren travels often with me, and we have our share of adventures. One time we were in one of the church sanctuaries by ourselves. Being the goofy girls we are, we started bouncing around on stage. We were doing every dance known to man and looking quite foolish. We left the sanctuary still laughing. Several people were talking in the foyer, and as we came by they stared at us; some of them laughed a little. We looked up, and I saw that a television camera recording the sanctuary had caught everything that went on and displayed it on

Lauren and I

a TV screen! Trying to cover up our embarrassment, we began laughing hysterically.

Another of my favorite parts about speaking in front of people is when I get to meet them afterward. Girls run up to me crying, telling me that their lives have been touched. Although telling the same story over and over again sometimes grows monotonous, every time I see someone's life touched supernaturally, it inspires me to keep going.

> ALL THAT I AM AND HAVE BECOME IS BECAUSE OF THE ONE INSIDE OF ME.

Sometimes I look back at my life and am awed. Every now and then, I have to reflect on my life and everything I have been through. With every trial and hard time, however, Jesus has stood by me the whole way through. Although I had to endure pain to get to my present state, I have learned that pain is the door to joy. People ask me if there is anything I would change about my life, and I have to answer no. Although I have my downfalls and shortcomings, God holds me in the palm of His hand. When I forsook Him, He did not forsake me. When I was scared, He comforted me. When I was alone, He dried my tears.

All that I am and have become is because of the One inside of me.

Chapter Six

LEARNING LIFE'S LESSONS

Looking back on my life, I see evidence of the maturing process that had to take place. Directly after receiving Christ, I wasn't ready to preach to others. I had to grow up spiritually. After every obstacle I overcame, there was a new one to climb. However, these adversities allowed me to grow. Holding on to the hand of Jesus as He walks you through life does not mean you will have an easy life. Looking back, I am thankful for every trial I had to go through because they helped make me who I am.

The Rejection Factor & the Making of Columbine Incidents

For most teenagers, high school is a time to have fun, make lots of friends—who you will never see after you graduate—and try to establish yourself for the future, which is usually not the most popular of the three. At some point, everyone has had to face rejection to some degree—from the boy no one wants to talk to at lunch to the popular girl who has seems to have it all together at school yet has a crummy life at home. Everyone faces rejection. This rejection can often lead to a misinterpretation of one's self and identity. Rejection causes walls to go up and can make people project false versions of themselves that they think others will accept more easily.

Growing up, I hated it. It stared me in the face every day. I began to feel insecure on the inside because I based my identity on what people said about me. My day would be good if I was complimented, bad if people made fun of me. My surroundings determined who I was. Insecurity brings out instability in a person, causing them to do things they know are wrong.

Everyone wants to be loved. People want to know that they are cared for and adored. When people say nasty things to you, it hurts, and sometimes it hurts so badly that action against that person seems necessary. Feelings of hatred can be stirred up, and some may hold grudges. It happens all the time, and everyone has experienced it. How does someone escape this? How can someone be truly comfortable with who they are?

Perhaps you are popular and very pretty. That is fine, but is that your identity? What if one day you were in a terrible car accident? Where would that leave you? Would you have anything left to offer? Or maybe it is your talent that makes you known. What if one day you could no longer perform? Rejection can come knocking on your door, and suddenly you are not as talented or pretty as you used to be.

So how can you overcome rejection?

For me, it took all of my friends abandoning me for me to finally wake up. I don't want you to have to take the same route, so allow me to prevent you from suffering a similar fate. Many would say that you should try to develop your self-esteem and self-image. I would have to disagree. I feel that as Christians we are to lose our identity and take up Christ's. I am not saying you lose your personality, but often people mean *pride* when they say *self-esteem*. There is a difference. When you look to yourself to be somebody, you'll fail, for pride goes before a fall. That is why you must look to Jesus for your identity and security.

When I finally realized that there is someone out there who loves me and accepts me for who I am, my life began to take on a whole new direction. I quit caring about what others' opinions were of me, because what mattered most was Christ's opinion. The devil will often try to lie to you by telling you you're ugly, that you are not good enough, and that you'll never make it. But God says differently! He says you are beautiful, that you can make it, and that you can do anything through Him.

How do I know? The Bible tells me so. It says that we are fearfully and wonderfully made. God took time to sculpt and craft you personally. You were made in the image of God. He looks down on you and says you are wonderful. Don't let someone's opinion result in your downfall! Let people say what they want to say—they are just people. But always remember what God says—and He says you are wonderful!

Don't allow rejection get to you, for it will only rob you of what God has for you. My life is a perfect example. I was so concerned about impressing my friends to avoid rejection that I began to lose my own identity. I began to take on the identity that my friends wanted me to have and was became someone I was not. Don't let this happen to you! If your friends aren't your friends because they like you the way you are, get new friends! Trust me, I know. I could have saved myself a lot of heartache if I had the guts to stand up to them. Either your friends are taking you up, or they are bringing you down. Get out of that situation as fast as you can! God has better things in store for you.

When you live as a Christian, you can expect to be rejected. Don't expect to be the most popular kid at school and have the most friends. Jesus told us that because they hated Him first, then they will also hate us. You must learn to find your identity in Christ, and He will never let you down. When everyone else has deserted you, He will be there. When you're rejected, He will be the one to accept you with open arms. His Word promises that He will never leave you nor forsake you. Therefore, invest your stock in the One that lasts.

What to do When Life Fails You

I am no stranger to tragedy. It has knocked on my door several times, and I am only in my late teens. Sometimes it has been hard to find the will to move on, yet something inside has left me no choice.

Time is no respecter of people; it keeps going, and when you need a break, it doesn't stop—it keeps ticking. You might see your best friends betray you or your faithful friends die—such things are facts of life.

There is a way to survive in this cruel world, but it isn't wrapped in the fancy package everyone had hoped for. The solution isn't a magic word that will make all your problems disappear, but it will give you a reason to continue on and a desire to face the next day. The answer is Jesus Christ.

> TRIALS SCULPT OUR CHARACTER AND ALLOW US TO BECOME STRONGER CHRISTIANS.

Perhaps pain isn't something that we can ask God to take from our lives. Trials sculpt our character and allow us to become stronger Christians. They teach us lessons that we can't learn from a textbook or a self-help tape.

I have learned that pain stretches you. It tests your character and what you're made of, and it shines light in the areas where you need growth. After I lost my friends, I went through a time of being lonely, but for once in my life I was able to take my eyes off myself and my desires and place them on God. Although the tragedy of losing my friends was what brought me the pain, through the pain I found Christ. If I had not lost my friends, I might not have found Jesus.

I have learned that pain can almost be a gift, because it helps make us into the people we ought to be. Because of the circumstances I have been through, I am more equipped to help others, because now I know how they feel. To live is to learn, and the more you go through, the more you learn.

In March of 2001 my dad died of cancer. He was a fighter. After having his spleen removed, the dad I knew as being strong turned into a lifeless, weak person. You could see the pain in his eyes. He suffered many sleepless nights because the pain was so great. Yet, as I heard him awake in his bed, he was not complaining about the pain but praying; he was not praying to God asking Him to take the pain away but was thanking God for being there with him.

The week he died, I had a speaking engagement in Indiana, and I was to be gone for a week speaking in schools and at rallies. My dad usually traveled with me, but he was too weak to go. Before I left, I made sure I said goodbye. He had just been brought home from the hospital and was lying still in his bed. I slowly crept into the room, my eyes on his limp figure. His eyes were sunken into his head. I walked beside the bed and whispered, "Dad." He turned his face towards me and smiled. "I have to go now."

He continued smiling as he struggled to speak. "Go get them," he said softly.

"I will."

"You're my pride and joy, you know."

By now tears were rolling down my cheeks. "I love you dad," I said as I hugged him goodbye. That was the last time I saw my dad before he died. He passed away as I was speaking in Indiana to five thousand teenagers.

It would have been easier if my dad had given up on his fight against cancer, because it would save him a lot of pain. But he fought. My mom told me that once the doctor approached her about my dad. He said that he was going to have to start him on a different medication to get rid of the remaining cancer. He went on to say that if he were anyone else, he would have just told them that their time is short so make the best of it, but not with my dad. The doctor knew my dad would fight.

My dad left a legacy as a fighter—he would not quit no matter what the circumstances. The last trip he spoke on, he was in a lot of pain. He was awaiting a surgery and had severe back pains, yet he still got up and spoke. When my dad fought, he fought not only with cancer; he also fought for the lives of many others. He did not let pain or disappointment stop him and continued to do what God wanted him to do. He changed many lives; even during the years he battled death.

Because of the tragedies in my life, including my dad's death and Columbine, I recognize God is a refuge and protector.

I know for a fact that there is a God, because I have seen what He can do. No one can tell me otherwise; I've been there. I saw Him protect me from armed gunmen, and I watched him give my dad joy and the strength to keep going. I've seen Him give *me* the courage to keep going.

There is something significant about the scars we carry. They speak louder than any words. Scars should be worn as medals of honor, because they say that one has survived a difficult fight. As Christians we are all fighters. All Christians are in God's army, yet some of us choose not to fight.

The trials I have gone through drive me closer to God instead of farther away from Him. I was recently in a serious relationship with a boy. We were in a strict courting relationship but believed we would one day marry. After being together for about nine months, he joined a Christian discipleship program. This program does not allow one to date or have any relationship with the opposite sex for nine months so that a person can seek God completely without any distractions. When he left, I grew very lonely. Because he still went to our church, I saw him often, but it was not the same. Although we promised to wait for each other, I still went through a lot of pain. In those times, I had some of my most intimate times with Jesus. If I had not gone through the pain, then I would have never experienced those crucial times with God.

Every trial we experience can craft us and make us more like Christ. Sometimes the only way we learn is through the trials of life, and that is why I believe the Bible says that suffering produces perseverance, and perseverance produces character, and character hope.

Sometimes people wonder, how could a good God allow suffering to continue? Although I believe that it was not God's ultimate plan for humans to suffer, I think that because He is good, He allows us to suffer. Just as a father disciplines a son, so our Heavenly Father allows us to undergo suffering. If a father never disciplined his son, then his son would be worse off for it.

Because the father knows what is best for his son, he sometimes permits a temporary pain in order to promote his son's growth. Suffering or pain should be thought of as a gift that enables us to grow up and be the people God wants us to be. Paul says to rejoice in our trials, because they allow God to teach us vital lessons in our life.

> WHEN GOING THROUGH A TRIAL, FOCUS ON JESUS AND NOT THE PAIN.

We must not be afraid of pain, because with pain comes triumph. You cannot have a victory unless you have a fight, and fighting often requires loss, pain, hardship, and disappointment. In order to get through the pain, it is important not to focus on the pain. When going through a trial, focus on Jesus and not the pain, and you will always get through. It helps me to know that one day every trial will be worth it when I hear the precious words of my Savior, "Well done good and faithful servant." The time will come when every tear will be wiped from our eyes, and we will never feel any pain at all. But until then we need to be soldiers of the cross. A great comfort is to know that what we see now is only a temporary state of existence, and one day we will be with the Lord.

One day everything will make sense and come together. You will see that every trial was for a reason, and you will be proud that you had them. Somehow the small battles are preparations for bigger battles. Once you've learned one thing, then something else comes up; this helps complete our faith. It is to liken us to Christ, and after becoming a Christian, that should be our main goal.

Job 23:10 says, "But He knows the way I take; when He has tested me I will come forth as gold." I believe it is important that this happens, because the more we become like Jesus, the more we will know Him. As we go through trials, we begin to understand Him better. There is a yearning in my soul to desire more of Him, and I have come to the point that if I must go through trials to know Him, I will do so gladly. God is faithful; His Word promises that He will not give us anything we cannot handle. He just wants us to really know Him and to experience Him, and that requires us to be shaped. And sometimes pain is the tool of choice for shaping us.

Whenever I go through a hard time, it is a great comfort to know that Jesus experienced all manners of trials and tribulations, and He knows how I feel. God is not just a distant ruler who doesn't care; He actually has been on our level and knows what it is like to hurt.

Jesus went through the same temptations we did, had the same needs we have, and felt the same pain we do—only worse. He went through the greatest pain anyone has ever been through when He took our sins away on the cross. So, we must never think that He has no idea what it feels like to hurt. If Jesus had not gone through the pain of the cross, we would not have salvation and would have no hope. His pain produced a victory that brought salvation to the world. Likewise, sometimes there is suffering we must endure to produce victories.

I sometimes think about what my suffering and the suffering of others produced. Although the Columbine tragedy was a horrific experience, I have seen many people changed for the better as a result of my testimony. Looking back, I can see the hand of God in my life, and I know that my personal pain was worth it.

In the short time I have lived, I have realized that things happen for a reason, though sometimes we do not know that reason. We must trust God and know that He will get us through. I know my God is faithful, and He will always get me through any trial and tribulation. His Word promises that we can do all things through Christ, so when things are rough it is important to rely on Jesus and His strength. We are a dependent people, and we need Jesus to carry us through.

If you are going through a hard time, do not turn to anything but Jesus.

PART II
THE MESSAGE

Now that I have given my testimony, you might want to know what I talk about when I go out and speak. My message varies depending on the audience, but for me everything comes down to loving God and loving people. Although I want to reach a lot of people in my life, I cannot reach them all.

The Bible says that if one can put a thousand to flight, two can put ten thousand to flight. God works in ways similar to a domino effect. One person can tell another person about Christ, and then the new person can reach another person for Christ and so on. My goal is to reach as many people as I can reach and to equip others to desire to do the same.

Throughout this second part, some sections are more appropriate for some people and other sections may be more important to other people due to the variety of people with whom I have had opportunities to share. Keep in mind that I am an ordinary teenager, and I'm often preaching to myself as well!

Chapter Seven

You Are Not Guaranteed a Tomorrow

Thirteen teens walked into Columbine High School thinking that they would come home as they would on any ordinary day, but they did not. Thousands of people are killed every year in car accidents. Who is to say that it won't be you? I am not trying to scare you into Christianity if you're not saved, but I don't apologize for telling you the truth. Sure, you can live your life as you normally do, having fun and carrying on. But death may come knocking on your door the next day. Are you ready? Now here comes the thought-provoking question: If you were to die today, where would you go? Heaven or hell?

In 2 Corinthians 6 at the bottom of the second verse it reads, "I tell you, now is the time of God's favor, now is the day of salvation." If you are reading this and have never asked Jesus to be your Lord and Savior or if you have slipped away from Christ, Jesus is saying to you now, "Today is the day of Salvation—don't wait any longer."

The Explanation

I don't know your story or what you are going through, but I do know that there is a God who cares. He is reaching down to your heart right now, desperately wanting to have a relationship with you. Allow me to define "relationship" in this context: You may attend church and go through the motions, even be a good person, and still might go to hell. Why? Because salvation is not knowing *about* God—it is *knowing* God. You may be able to quote the entire Bible or even put some Christians to shame with your good works, but that will do you no good if you don't know Jesus Christ.

The entire reason for the creation of mankind was so that God could have relationship. When Adam severed that relationship in Genesis, God had to find a way to restore it. Thousands of years later, Jesus was sent as God on earth to pay for the sins of the world through His death on the cross. On the third day He rose from the dead and defeated death by taking away the keys to hell and the grave. Because of

> SALVATION IS NOT KNOWING *ABOUT* GOD—IT IS *KNOWING GOD*.

His victory, we are invited to join with Him and live with Him for eternity. Now all those who accept Him by confessing Jesus as Lord with their mouth and believing in their heart that God raised Him from the dead will be saved.

Satan roams the world seeking whom he may devour. He is here to do nothing but steal, kill, and destroy by offering counterfeit hope. If you are living in the darkness, come to the light today. Jesus wants to give you life! Satisfaction is only found in Him; any other path will only lead to destruction.

The Bible says to taste and see that the Lord is good. As a person who has seen both sides of the fence and knows some of the pleasures that the world has to offer, I know for a fact that Jesus is the only way to go. My life has never been so good. The day I accepted Christ, all of my old wants and habits were changed by the blood of the Lamb, which is Jesus' sacrifice of Himself—the death of the perfect Lamb of God on the cross. I am not saying Christianity is easy, but the easy road is not always the best road.

Blessed Assurance

Senators everywhere are screaming for more protection in schools. They say that just one more gun law should do it; that if we put metal detectors in the schools, then kids will be safe; and that we need more policemen in our schools. The problem with these statements is found in Psalm 127:1: "Unless the Lord builds the house, its builders labor in vain. Unless the Lord watches over the city, the watchmen stand guard in vain." (NIV). We can try to take away the guns, failing to realize that when Dillan and Eric walked into Columbine, they were breaking twenty-one gun laws, and we can try to put more policemen on guard, but there were a thousand policemen at Columbine on April 20.

Several times I have been asked what assurance I can give to kids going back to schools. The truth is, there is no assurance except Jesus Christ. Columbine was located in a good part of town. There were no gang problems or any crime problems. Until the shooting happened, the biggest news our community received was when a nearby McDonald's was robbed. Columbine High School had one of the best reputations in the state; it was high in athletics and high in academics. Teenagers always felt safe going there.

The point? If it could happen in my community, it could happen in yours. Now don't go ballistic; I'm just telling you the truth. I think that there needs to be more awareness. The good news, however, is that when you know Christ as your Lord and personal Savior, He holds your future in the palm of His hand. He offers His perfect love that casts away all fear. Let's look at Psalm 91, one of my favorite Psalms.

> He who dwells in the shelter of the Most High will rest in the shadow of the Almighty. I will say of the Lord, "He is my refuge and my fortress, my God, in whom I trust." Surely he will save you from the fowler's snare and from the deadly pestilence. He will cover you with His feathers, and

under his wings you will find refuge; his faithfulness will be your shield and rampart. You will not fear the terror of night, nor the arrow that flies by day, nor the pestilence that stalks in the darkness, nor the plague that destroys at midday. A thousand may fall at your side, ten thousand at your right hand, but it will not come near you. You will only observe with your eyes and see the punishment of the wicked. If you make the Most High your dwelling—even the Lord, who is my refuge— then no harm will befall you , no disaster will come near your tent. For He will command his angels concerning you to guard you in all your ways; they will lift you up in their hands, so that you will not strike your foot against a stone. You will tread upon the lion and the cobra; you will trample the great lion and the serpent. "Because he loves me," says the Lord, "I will rescue him; I will protect him for he acknowledges my name. He will call upon me, and I will answer him; I will be with him in trouble. I will deliver him and honor him. With long life will I satisfy him and show him my salvation.

Maybe you are scared to send your kids to school or maybe you're a teenager who is scared to go to school. As American morals keep diminishing, the only hope is Jesus. Hope is not found in daily horoscopes, shots of tequila, or your best friend. People can turn to their therapists for help, doctors when they are sick, pills when they are depressed, rehab when they are drunk,

> HOPE IS NOT FOUND IN DAILY HOROSCOPES, SHOTS OF TEQUILA, OR YOUR BEST FRIEND. . . HOPE IS FOUND IN JESUS.

sex when they are lonely, crime when they are hurt, drugs when they're scared, but this only puts a Band-Aid on the problem. Hope is found in Jesus. The Bible says in Romans 8: 24 that hope that is seen is no hope at all.

Don't wait and hope that things will get better. If you don't know Christ, He is reaching out hope to you today. He is pursuing you with His love. It is true that there is a heaven, and there is a hell. Those that do not know Christ will go to hell. Don't wait for tomorrow, for you don't know what tomorrow holds.

Fear

Everyone has fear—fear of death, fear of flying, fear of heights, fear of sickness, fear of spiders . . . Where does fear come from? The Bible says that God has not given us a spirit of fear but love power and a sound mind. Therefore, fear is from Satan himself. He feels that if he can get Christians to fear something, then he can keep them from doing what God has called them to do.

I have had to overcome many fears in my life. For instance, I was not always a public speaker. I would get nervous when I had to speak in front of ten people, yet in order for God to use me, I had to conqueror my fear of public speaking. Had I not conquered that fear then, many lives that I have touched through my message may not have come to know Christ. Fear paralyzes you from accomplishing what God has chosen for you to accomplish. In Luke 12:4-6 it says:

> "I tell you, my friends, do not be afraid of those who kill the body and after that can do no more. But I will show you whom you should fear: Fear him who, after the killing of the body, has power to throw you into hell. Yes, I tell you, fear him. Are not five sparrows sold for two pennies? Yet not one of them is forgotten by God. Indeed, the very hairs of your head are all numbered.

Don't be afraid; you are worth more than many sparrows. *"*

Christ has come to deliver you from fear, because when His love reaches your heart, it drives fear away.

Preparing for Eternity

Sometimes we get caught in the "now." People have a tendency to be concerned only about their life on earth. Well, I have got news for you: eternity is much longer than your life spent on earth. The Bible describes life as a vapor. Life quickly passes away. The Bible warns us to store up our treasures in heaven where it cannot be destroyed, because where your treasure is, there your heart will be. What plans are you making for eternity? What you did on earth will affect your eternity. If you are not living for Christ, eternity is a long time to go without Him.

Chapter Eight

THE PEOPLE AROUND YOU AREN'T GUARANTEED A TOMORROW EITHER

Matthew 28:19-20 says,

> "Therefore go and make disciples of all nations, baptizing them in the name of the Father and of the Son and of the Holy Spirit, and teaching them to obey everything I have commanded you. And surely I am with you always, to the very end of the age."

If you have been born again, saved, and set free—guess what? It doesn't stop there! Common sense says that there are more non-Christians then Christians in the world today. Because we as Christians have been given the best gift in the entire world, it is time we now share that gift. Many times Christians hide their light or try to cover it up when it is that very light that could save an entire generation.

Some Christians walk around as recluses, not letting even their close friends know about Jesus. Well, I hope they get their act together before Judgment Day! Personally, when I go to heaven I don't want Jesus to have to ask me why I didn't reach out to certain people. I don't want there to be even one person that I could have reached and didn't. "Why," you ask? Because every day people die and go to hell. Hell is real, but somehow people allow things to get in the way of reaching out to people that need to be touched. It is time we become like Jesus who made Himself of no reputation for people. If we do not become the light that God has commissioned us to become, then who will be it? The Mormons? The Hindus? The alcoholic on the corner? We are the light of the world. God chose to use us to accomplish His work and to spread His Gospel. Will we rise up to the challenge of touching this generation, or will we continue to see people die and go to hell because someone did not have the guts to tell them about Jesus?

The Bible says that the harvest is ripe but the workers are few. Will you join with me in reaping the harvest?

How to Develop the Passion

Paul stated that he was crucified with Christ and no longer lived, but Christ lived within Him. 2 Corinthians 5:17 says, "If anyone is in Christ, he is a new creation; the old has gone, the new has come!" When you accept Christ, you die to yourself. This simply means you quit living your life for your wants, for your flesh, and for your old nature. Because *you* are "dead," Christ lives in you, meaning you have His wants, His desires, and His thoughts.

> "IF ANYONE IS IN CHRIST, HE IS A NEW CREATION; THE OLD HAS GONE, AND THE NEW HAS COME."
> 2 CORINTHIANS 5:17

I believe this is all done as a process—a process known as sanctification in which Christians become more Christ-like. His thoughts start becoming your thoughts, and His wants start becoming your wants. As we are sanctified and made more like Christ, we begin to see things the way He sees things, feel the way He feels, and cry for the things for which He cries.

The Bible says that Jesus came to seek and save the lost. Jesus tells a parable in the Bible about how a shepherd would leave ninety-nine sheep to just rescue one that was lost. Now that's passion! Jesus cares deeply about those who don't know Him. He wants all to repent and none to perish. His love for the lost took Him to the cross, where He suffered a terrible death. He died because He knew that it was the only way to reconcile God and man. He was ripped apart so that people can have fellowship with God—the way it was meant to be. Jesus cares about every lost sheep, and now that He is in heaven, seated at the right hand of God, He has chosen us to reach out to those lost sheep. His last words before ascending into heaven were about reaching the lost sheep of the world.

Now if we become sanctified and become more and more like Jesus, we will have the same desires He has—to reach as many people as is possible and not miss one. The Bible says that God desires all to come to repentance. It is time to start proclaiming the Good News!

Before Jesus died, He prayed in the Garden of Gethsemane. He prayed that He might be one with His disciples. While thinking on this scripture, I realized that He meant that He wanted His creation to have His wants and desires because by being of one mind and goal.

Intimacy with Christ is key. If we wish to reach the lost, we must know the person for whom we are reaching them. It is much easier to tell them about someone we know personally and spend time with than someone we only know about. Quiet times spent with Jesus will reflect your level of influence in someone's life. The more you spend with Him and learn to fall in love with Him, you will desire to do His will and not your own as Jesus stated to His heavenly Father when He said, "Not my will but yours be done." By reading the Word, we will begin to see His will is to reach out to those who don't know Him personally and intimately. Sure, we may get laughed at, made fun of, and despised, but what are those trials in comparison to the joy of giving someone the opportunity to know someone that could change their life forever?

Sad Facts

We live in a hurting world plagued by the disease of sin. Having been given the remedy, we spread the cure among the world's unbelievers. One look at the streets of any major city will show the hurt and pain in our world. People are crying out for answers, yet few Christians ever reveal them.

Jesus is the only answer! While people are searching for solace in their horoscopes or whiskey bottles, hope is just around the corner. As Christians, we hold the potential to change our world, yet we often let little things get in the way. It is time we lay down our reputations and pride and do what God has called every Christian to do—preach the Good News.

Why Reach Out?

Many teenagers and adults are deeply hurting. How do I know? Over five hundred thousand teenagers try to commit suicide a year. There has to be a problem when every day teens turn toward sex, violence, drugs, and alcohol; yet many Christians simply feel badly about their plight and yet do nothing about it. Christians need to become more proactive.

Let's put it in perspective. The Bible says that Jesus came to seek and save the lost. After salvation, one will undergo the process of sanctification, which is God conforming the person to become like Him. Soon that person, if he or she is spending intimate time with God and getting to know Him, will develop His wants and His desires. And the whole reason that Christ came was to bring as many people with Him to the Father as will come with Him.

When God looks down on His creation, He loves it. He loves each and every person and longs to have fellowship with him or her, and He has chosen us to reach them for Him. He has called us to reach out to people with His love by preaching the Gospel, the Good News. Jesus said that we are the salt of the earth and the light in the darkness. We are commissioned by the Word of God to go!

Jesus gave us two commandments: Love the Lord with all of your heart, soul, and mind; and love your neighbor as yourself. My personal prayer request is that I might love people with the same love that Jesus has for them-love that's slow to anger and full of compassion.

I don't want to walk by one person that I could have reached but did not. It is not because I want to add that person to my "list," so to speak. My main motive for reaching others isn't to make me look like a good person. I want to develop the same love that Jesus had for people, where I cannot stand the fact that people are dying without knowing a better way.

The brutal truth is that if we don't share the love of Jesus, people will die and go to hell. I don't want someone else's blood on my hands. We may be the only evidence of Jesus that someone will ever see. It is time we start letting our lights shine.

Agape Love

Think of Jesus—He was willing to lay everything down. He paid the ultimate price to redeem us from our sins. As Christians, we have the same calling—to lay our lives down for others. The Bible says in John 15:13, "Greater love has no man than this, that he lay down his life for his friends." I wish to have the same love that Jesus had when they nailed Him to the cross.

I sincerely believe that as we draw closer to the heart of the Father, we will begin to see His heart crying out to the lost people. We will begin to see His heart reaching out to the ugliest people, wanting desparately to have a relationship with His creation. As we draw near to God and come to know Him, He will make us more like Himself. The love that He has for His creation will then begin to grow inside us as we, too, desire to reach the people who do not know Christ.

I desire to have the kind of love Jesus had. We often have a way of looking or judging someone's heart based on how they look on the outside. In I Samuel 16:7, the Bible says that man looks at the outward appearance of man, but God looks at the heart. Jesus sat and ate with tax collectors and prostitutes—the scum of His day. The Pharisees mocked Him, but their taunts didn't get to Him. Many times, we can act like the Pharisees more than like Jesus. We don't see the person with long blue hair and a nose ring as being a person but more as a thing. Jesus brought Himself down to the level of peasants and the untouchables, not caring how they looked or how they behaved. I'm sure that many of those men smoked, drank, and cursed, but that didn't bother Jesus. Although we Christians must guard our hearts from becoming more worldly, we are not to isolate ourselves from the world. As Christians, we must not be afraid to get our hands dirty reaching out to the needy. We must do as Jesus did by becoming the least of all—ones that are even willing to serve servants.

The Bible says that the world will know us by our love. It is time Christians pop their bubbles and start loving the way Jesus did. This requires us to lay our lives down and serve other people.

One of my mentors told me about what happened to her when she was a teenager. She went to a Christian school where they frequently had chapel services in which guest speakers would come and preach. On one occasion, a man told the story of how he had banished a young woman who was dressed "inappropriately" for church. She was wearing a miniskirt and a half-top, and he told the woman to come back when she was completely dressed. After hearing this story, my friend was mad and left the chapel. The preacher later recognized my friend and approached her to find out why she had chosen to leave. She simply asked him the question, "Did the girl you kicked out ever come back to your church?" The preacher shook his head.

It is vital that we do not have a "holier than thou" attitude toward the world. Author Ray Comfort said that we should stop complaining about the sins of the world and start confronting them in his book *How to Win Souls and Influence People*. Christians are called to be in the world and not of it. Fellow Christians, it is time that we start being more Christ-like; He was willing to hang out with the people with whom no one else wanted to associate. Our love should be blind.

Students, be the one who will sit with someone no one else sits with at lunch. Be the one to accept someone that no one else will accept. I know it is easy to fall into the popularity trap in high school, but popularity is something that is insignificant next to following the call of Christ. If we want to see any change in this world, we must truly learn how to love people.

> IF WE WANT TO SEE ANY CHANGE IN THIS WORLD, WE MUST TRULY LEARN HOW TO LOVE PEOPLE.

I want to have the eyes of Christ so that I do not judge people by man's standards. I don't want to see a hooker as just a hooker but instead as someone who is hurting, looking for love, and just needs Jesus. I don't want to see an alcoholic as just an alcoholic but as someone who is trapped by an addiction and needs Jesus to free him. I don't want to see a homosexual as just being gay but as someone who is caught up in sin and does not know Jesus. We must stop looking down on sinners and start having real, Godly, agape love—the love that Jesus showed.

More Than Hell

Many people think that the most important reason to reach the lost is to prevent them from dying and going to hell. This is important, since hell is very real and very serious, but notice that when Jesus sent out His disciples, He did not mention hell. Jesus did not say, "Go and make disciples so that they will not go to hell." He just said, "Go and make disciples of all the nations." I believe there is much more to knowing Christ than not going to hell, and it is important that as Christians we are careful about how we talk about such a place.

One time I was witnessing to a girl in one of my classes. She was going off about how tired she was of hearing that if she didn't go to church, she would go to hell. Trying to be loving but firm, I explained to her how she was wrong, that church attendance was not the issue. I explained the love of Christ and how He died for her and wants a relationship with her. I also told her that there was hell and warned her not to wait to accept Jesus.

Christians often leave out part of the message. I believe that Jesus saved us from more than just hell. He saved us from our own nature. We are not free because we go to heaven; we are free because God rescued us from the law of sin and death. Knowing Jesus is much more than avoiding hell. He came to bind up the broken hearted, set the captives free, and bring life! The lost people in the world not only need Jesus to save them from Hell, they also need Him to set them free from their own nature and bring freedom. It is important that we portray both sides of Christ. He is a God of love and also a God of judgment.

Praying for the Lost

As a senior in high school, I got together with a few other people every day before school started in order to pray. This began as a result of See You at the Pole. I had explained to my

youth group that I felt that we should pray more than just one day of the year. I also enjoyed meeting every morning as a statement to the government; if they told me not to pray in school, I wanted to do so anyway. I thank the Lord for my sisters, who came with me

my sisters and I (Holly, me, & Heather)

every morning to agree with me in prayer for a change in our school. We believed that anything we asked in the name of Jesus would be done, so we prayed for lives to be touched at our school. Many times after we prayed, opportunities came up for us to witness to people; I believe that they were answers to prayer.

The Bible says that we have not because we asked not. We must be willing to take the time to pray. I am not saying that that's all we should ever do as Christians. We must, however, be prepared to stand in the gap on other people's behalf. Through prayer, we help to defeat the enemy's schemes and release the power of the Holy Spirit into a person. No person is brought to Christ without the work of the Holy Spirit, and Jesus says that our Father in heaven will readily give the Holy Spirit to those who ask.

Jesus to the World

After returning to a public school my senior year, I saw many people from all walks of life. It was hard for me to hear conversations going on in the hallway because profanity and sexual jokes filled the air. I witnessed teens proclaiming to be Christians acting just the same as those who didn't. It broke my heart. I silently cried, *If they only knew Jesus!* The fact is, however, that many of them did not want to know Jesus—at least the Jesus portrayed by most Christians they knew—the Jesus that says, "You are not going to heaven if you don't go to church every Sunday," or "If you don't follow this list of rules, then you are not worthy," or "Being a Christian means you don't have any fun."

It is time we start representing our Savior accurately. The world looks at the Church and sees hypocrisy and mediocrity. It is time we prove them wrong! We need to take up the unconditional love of Jesus Christ, which is willing to do anything so that someone else can be saved. We must show the world what it really means to be a Christian!

I believe that there would be more Christians today if we would start representing Jesus the way He should be represented. Personally, I pray that people would not even see me but instead see Him inside of me. I want my eyes to be as His, to have the same love, compassion, and kindness He portrayed. We are to *be*

Jesus to this world. We are to show them why they, too, should be Christians instead of driving them away. If we ever want to see our nation changed, then we must start taking on the attitudes of Jesus Christ. If you do not know what that looks like, the New Testament is an excellent resource.

Chapter Nine

TIME FOR A REVOLUTION

2 Chronicles 7:14 says,

> "If my people, who are called by my name, will humble themselves and pray and seek my face and turn from their wicked ways, then I will hear from heaven and will forgive their sin and will heal their land."

How badly do you want to see America changed? Is it something you crave and cry out for in the night, or is it something that seems too out of reach to ever take place? The promises of God say that if we seek Him and His ways by praying and turning from our wicked, selfish ways, then He will touch our land and heal it.

Look at America. It has everything to offer: fame, success, money, sex. Anything you want, America has—it's the land of opportunity. Yet it's a paradox; it claims to be the land of the free, and yet it is not free.

So what is freedom? Is freedom being allowed to do whatever you want? That's not freedom. Yes, it creates the *illusion* of freedom, but that is not what freedom is. The Bible says that Jesus came to set the captives free. Sin is not freedom. Sin is slavery, but the Bible says that he whom the Son sets free is free indeed. Knowing Jesus is freedom, for God has set us free from the law of sin and death.

Blood trickled down a wooden cross two thousand years ago to bring us freedom. America is not a free nation. It claims to be, but Satan and sin bind many people. It is time for America to truly be a free nation. Not just a feel—good freedom but the everlasting spiritual freedom only Jesus can bring—freedom from sin!

You are deceiving yourself if you choose to ignore America's downward spiral. Thank God there is hope! Christians, now is the time to come together and fight for our land to win it back!

Time to Fight

Hundreds of years ago, a war was fought in America known as the Revolutionary War. The purpose of this war was both simple and complicated—freedom. Now is time for American Christians to fight the same battle for that same glorious purpose only this time it is for spiritual freedom

Many soldiers died knowing that it was better to die than remain in chains. We, too, must have the same passion, pursuing our country's freedom, even to the grave. If America's freedom is worth fighting for, then lets fight! We don't know how much more time is left. So let's fight. America needs us if it is ever going to be a truly free country.

I don't want any more shootings to happen. I don't want any more people to die. If we Christians do not start standing up and fighting the devil for our nation, more deaths are inevitable.

God has promised to heal our land, but we have got to be willing to do what He has asked us to do. The biggest single factor that holds back revival in America is the Christians. We have let the devil rob us of what is rightfully ours—let's get it back!

Obey God

They took prayer out of schools, and just as Richard Wormbrand, a pastor from Romania, I ask, "Why did we listen?" We have allowed the government to have more say in our lives than the God of all creation. I believe in honoring those in authority but not when it contradicts what Jesus has told us to do. He is our supreme ruler, not the government. Although the government may tell you to not pray in school, Jesus says to pray. To whom do you listen?

America is covered with lukewarm Christians who are afraid to take a stand. If this continues, America has no hope. People that are passionate for God are hard to find. It is sad when the Christians cannot be picked out from the non-Christians, it is not due to fact that the world is becoming more godly—Christians are becoming more like the world.

We have become lazy in our walk and duties. In America we have been blessed tremendously, and as people are martyred around the world daily, we are too afraid to take a stand in our public schools by praying. Come on Christians, what will it take for us to begin to realize that if we forget about our material well-being and reputation, then we will begin to see revival?

Revival

Practically every Christian wants revival. We sing songs in church such as "Revival Fire Fall." We plead and plead, and I believe God has answered us—just probably not the way we had hoped. If we want to see revival in our nation, we must allow revival to take place in our hearts. Once we let the Holy Spirit take complete control, then we will see revival.

> WE KEEP "NO TRESPASSING" SIGNS OVER CERTAIN AREAS OF OUR HEARTS.

I was recently at a conference with several well-know preachers. It was an awesome time, and I saw many people get delivered and healed. Pastor David Ravenhill was there from England, and he said that the reason there is no revival in America today is that we deny Jesus His lordship over our lives. In other words, he was saying we keep little "no trespassing" signs over certain areas of hearts, allowing us to love Jesus with only 99.9 percent of our heart.

The Bible, however, commands us to love the Lord with *all* of our heart, soul, and mind. If we want the world to experience the Spirit of God taking over by storm, then we have got to allow Him to take over our lives first. We have to allow ourselves to be completely abandoned to Him so that we are willing to do anything just to be with Him. My prayer to Jesus is that I want to learn to love Him just as much as He loves me. Our main goal in life shouldn't be to win the most souls, heal the most people, or pray the most. Our goal in life should become falling so in love with Jesus Christ that we would be willing to do anything He asks of us. Once Christians reach that point in their lives, we will see revival.

The Cost

Jesus instructs us to pick up our cross and follow Him. The Bible says that if you put your hand to the plow and look back, you are not worthy of God's kingdom. The way of Jesus is not "the easy life." The Bible says that the road is narrow and few will choose to take it. Christianity is not necessarily easy when you are living the life of a *true* Christian.

Consider the lives of the disciples. All but one died because of their faith. The cause of the gospel cost them everything, yet because of their efforts our church and Christianity are what they are today.

Paul went through many trials as a Christian. He was put into chains for Christ, beaten for Christ, and eventually died for Christ. Although he had everything coming against Him and had every reason to quit preaching the Gospel, he kept fighting. Even when he was locked in a jail cell before his set execution time, he praised God along with Silas. He was so passionate about Jesus that he was willing to go through anything. In Philippines 3:7-8 he writes, "But whatever was to my profit I now consider loss for the sake of Christ. What is more, I consider everything a loss compared to the surpassing greatness of knowing Christ Jesus my Lord, for whose sake I have lost all things."

Jesus requires everything of us, and the cost of being a Christian is laying our lives down. John the Baptist said, "I must decrease that He may increase." We must choose to put our lives second so that Jesus may live inside of us and do big things through us.

Jesus said to pick up your cross, and the way of the cross is often a way of pain. Think of the pain it caused Jesus to walk to Golgatha with the crown of thorns upon His brow and the agony it caused Him as the splintering cross pierced His freshly beaten back. Are you ready for the cross? Although the Christian life may not be easy, it is by far the noblest life one could lead. Remember, our rewards are in heaven and not in this life!

Our Enemy

Satan is out to steal, kill and destroy. He roams the earth like a lion seeking whom he may devour. The moment you are saved, you become his enemy. The more you make him mad, the more he hates you. But the good news is that he was defeated by Jesus' death on the cross! Just as Jesus overcame the world, so can we. Sometimes, however, we behave as though we are the ones that lost! We allow Satan to have his way in our lives by giving in to our selfish desires. We forget that we are supposed to be fighting him and that he's already been defeated!

Many people even try to make friends with Satan—while they say they're Christians! Christians sometimes look for an excuse to sin. They try to find loopholes that will allow them to continue sinning without consequence.

Christians, it is time for us to be *violent*—spiritually that is. Satan has trampled around our land and has stolen what is rightfully ours. And we let him. They took prayer out of schools and many Christians said nothing. They made abortion legal and many did not complain. Instead of being so tolerant, we must be aggressive. Satan had no right to take prayer out of our schools, so let's get it back!

The Bible says that our battle is not against people, but instead it is against Satan and his demons. Satan knows his time is short on earth, so he is trying to make the best of it. He has declared an all-out war against God and is trying all the tricks in his arsenal to bring as many people to hell with him as he can. We shouldn't let him have *one*! The Bible says that we are greater. ("Greater is he that is in you, than he that is in the world"). We have authority over him, so let's take it and fight for what is ours. It does not matter how young or old we are; we are all called to fight against the enemy. It looks like Satan is winning the war in America, and many Christians are letting him.

Attack from the Enemy

Smith Wiggelsworth said, "If you don't have any trials, it means you are not worth them." How well does hell know your name? Some Christians face no enemy attack because they pose no threat. They are not doing anything that would stir up the demons in hell, so Satan does not even choose to bother them. If you fight against hell, it will fight you back; but if you are doing absolutely nothing to make them mad, Satan and his demons will leave you alone— laughing as they drag people to hell.

> YOU MAKE HELL MAD EVERY TIME YOU DO SOMETHING FOR GOD.

You make hell mad every time you do something for God, every time you reach out to another person, every time you pray in spiritual warfare, and every time you fulfill the call of God on your life. Making the devil mad should be something we do on a regular basis. We should make him so mad that he would do everything in his power to stop us—because we know that God has the greater power and by the name of Jesus every knee shall bow in heaven and on earth.

Some of you are probably asking, what's the point? Why should I want to make the devil mad at me? The answer is that every time you do something that makes him mad, it means you are doing something right for God. The good news, however, is that although you make him mad, there is only so much he can do. If it were up to Satan, he would annihilate us all; but his desires must fall into the will of God. He can't do anything to you unless he has God's permission first. Therefore, there is nothing that we should fear about him, for he is no threat to us as long as we go with Christ!

What Will People Say About You?

If you were to die right now, what would be your legacy? What would people say about you? For what would you be known? Would you be known for how well you partied or for how stylishly you got around town? Think about these questions carefully, and if you don't like your answer, change it while you still can!

It is important that you realize the potential you carry. When you grab on to what God has for you, there is nothing you can't do. You can make history! Right now, America is headed in the wrong direction—so let's change it back to its right course. We can do all things through Christ who strengthens us, because God is a God of the impossible. Smith Wiggelsworth said, "All things are possible if you dare to believe." Let's dare to believe that one day America will be worthy of being called a Christian nation again and that we have not yet seen the greatest revival ever. Let's believe that America's youth will no longer be an X or Y generation but a revival generation! Let's believe the impossible, because when we begin to believe the impossible, the impossible will begin to take place.

Let's start a revolution!

Chapter Ten

IN MY SHOES

April 20, 1999—a day known around the world for tragedy. Two seniors opened fire at Columbine High School, killing eleven students and one teacher. The damage, however, was minimal in comparison to the gunmen's ultimate plan. Located directly underneath the library in the school's cafeteria was a propane-tank bomb, set to go off and kill over five hundred students. Fortunately, a couple of wires were crossed—preventing the explosion. Besides bringing the two bombs, the gunmen carried two guns each and several small explosives. Decked out in trench coats and strapped with artillery, they came prepared to kill as many students as they could. At 11:21 in the morning, the worst school shooting in American history took place.

And I was in the heart of it.

The Columbine massacre caused many to question important issues such as, "What if Columbine happened in my school?" or "What is wrong with a nation that kills her own children?" Not only did Columbine touch the small area of Littleton, Colorado, it literally reached people around the world.

Having gone through Columbine, I had to ask myself several difficult questions relating to my own life. Now it is your turn to ask yourself the hard questions learned from a tragedy.

1.   Pretend that you were in my position—you're working on your homework when someone comes running in, yelling that someone has been shot. What would be the first thing that would go through your head?

_____

_____

_____

_____

2.   Now that you're under a desk, you hear a loud explosion—a pipe bomb has just gone off outside the library, and the air is beginning to fill with smoke. Two dark figures enter the library and begin shouting, "Get ready to die!" What do you think would be going through your mind if you found yourself here? What if you're the next one to die? Are you ready? Why or why not?

_____

_____

_____

_____

3.   Although chaos surrounded me, I had an inner peace because I knew Jesus. Two months before the shooting took place, I had dedicated my heart to Him. I knew beyond a shadow of a doubt that I would go to heaven instead of hell if I were to die. I did not have this reassurance because I attended church regularly (which I did), because I was a good person, or because I had followed a list of rules. I had peace because I had something real living inside of me—I had turned my back on sin and the way I had been living, and I had fallen in love with Jesus. As thoughts of losing my life ran though my head, I knew that whether I lived or died, I would be okay.

Would you have any doubts as to your eternal destination? If so, why or why not? Do you remember where you were when you dedicated your life to God? If not, perhaps you'd like to do so now.

---

4. Still shaking violently, you get up from under your table. You see one of your friends helping out a wounded girl who has had her shoulder blown off. Somehow they missed you and their bombs didn't go off—you're still alive, somehow!

Pretend you just got out of a life-threatening situation. What kind of thoughts would be going though your mind? You've been miraculously spared while others have died violent, painful deaths. Picture it in your mind, and ask yourself how that would make you feel.

---

5. We were brought to a neighborhood, which was located close to the school. There we would wait until our parents could pick us up. Consequently, there were several obstacles which made it harder for parents to reach their children. Several main streets were blocked off, keeping parents locked outside of the neighborhoods. I finally met my parents around five o'clock that night.

Because of the emergency vehicle activity and security precautions, your family is unable to reach you for hours and hours. In the meantime, you're stranded at the home of a complete stranger, having just lived through the most traumatic event of your entire life. How would you feel the first time you saw your family and the ones you love?

---

6.   It wasn't until the day after the tragedy that I heard that I had lost one of my best friends, Rachel. She had been a Christian and had died professing her faith. Because of her legacy, many have come to know Christ through her life as well as her death.

If you died today what would you be remembered for? What would people say about you?

_____

_____

_____

_____

If you do not like your answers to the above questions, change them while you still can! You do not know how long you have on this earth. It's important to know where you stand. If your life is not right with Jesus Christ, get right today! Thirteen people walked into Columbine that day thinking they would have a normal day—that day they would be able to go home to their parents, hang out with their friends, or accomplish their dreams. Thirteen people who walked in that day did not walk out. Maybe you are a Christian, but you aren't living completely for Jesus. Change your life while you still can! You only have one chance to live, one chance to make a difference, one chance to live for Jesus. Do not waste your life away! I tell you that Jesus loves you and wants the best for you. Don't wait another second! Life is too short.

Chapter Eleven

AFTER COLUMBINE

Suddenly my world had fallen. There were broken pieces of my heart that needed to be put back together. Columbine was something that no one knew was coming, and therefore, they were unprepared for it. In order to make it through, I needed something bigger than myself or I wouldn't have made it. God fit that description.

1. How would you try to cope with events like the Columbine shooting if you were in my position? What would be the first thing you would do? Would you have any short- or long-term goals? How would being a survivor affect your later life?

_____

_____

_____

_____

2. Can you think of something that you might do for a friend who has been through something tragic—even if it wasn't this tragic—using personal insight from the previous question?

_____

_____

_____

_____

In that time of desperation, I was so grateful that I had Jesus Christ. He's promised to never leave or forsake us. He held me when I was scared and wiped my tears when I was crying. He understood me when no one else could. Because of Him, I made it through the hard times.

3. Can you remember a difficult time you've gone through? What would it have been like if you had had an active relationship with Jesus to help see you through?

_____

_____

_____

_____

4. Although I was blessed to have no severe flashbacks or nightmares, I was still afraid. After two weeks, we went back to school. Because the damage to Columbine was so great, we were forced to use a different facility. For one month we attended our rival school, Chattfield. The school was very noisy; a door would slam and it would sound like a gun. This left me on edge.

When I was scared at school, I learned to rely on God. I would pray silently and say Bible verses over and over in my head. Although it was a hard time, God brought me through. His grace was there to keep me from fear and to help me deal with the situation I witnessed. Not only was He there for me April 20, 1999, He has been there every day since and walks me along with my hand in His.

What are some things that help you when you're on edge and afraid? How would it make you feel if you knew that your heavenly Father has a plan for your life? Would knowing this make dealing with persistent fear easier?

_____

_____

_____

_____

5. I began speaking in churches and other venues about Columbine a month after it happened. As I spoke and had the

Heidi Johnson

opportunity to reach others, I was also being reached. What was meant for evil, God turned to good as He promised in His Word.

Several precious lives were lost at Columbine, but in the aftermath, people's lives are being changed.

What is something bad that has happened to you that you could use to help others? What is a lesson you learned from one of your mistakes that you could use to keep others from doing the same thing?

_____

_____

_____

_____

Maybe you have gone through some rough times or are currently going through a trial or tribulation. I want to let you know that God cares for you and is there for you—if you will let Him. Sometimes we cannot understand all that happens, but we can understand that there is a God who cares and has our best interest at heart. All we need to do is put our hope and trust in Him.

89

Chapter Twelve

HOW TO PREVENT MORE COLUMBINES FROM HAPPENING

Many lessons were learned from Columbine. Because of the tragedy, our nation began to realize that something is wrong with public schools where teenagers are killing their own in school. Since Columbine, many other copycat activities have taken place and several schools have been threatened.

You have the power to personally prevent shootings from happening. Teenagers, if you hear anyone saying directly that they are planning any form of violent act in your school, you are responsible to go straight to a teacher, principal, counselor, or law-enforcement agent and report what you have heard. You hear and see what is going on in your school more than anyone else does; therefore, you have the ability to make your school safe.

1. List as many ways and ideas as you can think of to make your school safer. How do you think depression and lack of self-worth affected the Columbine gunmen? Review chapter six's section on rejection and use those thoughts to guide your brainstorming!

_____

_____

_____

_____

2. You can also prevent violence by reaching out to people outside your comfort zone. How?

_____

---

3. As I mentioned earlier, I was recently speaking at a public school in Indiana where a boy who desperately wanted to talk later approached me. After a good part of the crowd had left, I sat down and talked with him. He told me how he was picked on all the time and felt he couldn't take it any more, and was considering causing a shooting in his school. This boy just wanted people to be nice to him; he was tired of being an outcast and an outsider.

How do you think Jesus would have treated this boy? How do you think you as a Christian could influence his feelings of rejection—especially since, as a Christian, you serve a God—who loves all mankind enough to die for us on a cross?

---

4. Many people are asking why Columbine happened. If we can find out what causes violent behavior, then maybe we can prevent it. Americans are looking for easy answers to cover up the problem. Well, I have the easiest answer yet—Jesus! Until people meet Him and know His love, Columbines will continue to happen. He is the only One who can really heal a broken heart or turn hate into love. If you are a Christian, you have a responsibility.

List ways you can reach out in your school. Keep in mind that you don't have to have government funding or a globe-spanning ministry to reach lost souls. What can *you* do to reach the hurting people of your school *every day*?

_____

_____

5. List some people's names that you can reach out to in your school (don't always go for the easy people). What kinds of changes might a relationship with the all-loving Father God make in their lives?

_____

_____

_____

_____

Final Words

Life is precious; it comes and goes like the wind. I challenge you to look at your life before you move on from this book. What is the meaning of your life? Are you making a difference? Maybe you want to have a meaningful life and leave a legacy but don't know where to start. Jesus is the only One who can bring true meaning and purpose to your life.

God is not looking for perfect people, and He is not looking for someone who has everything all together. He is looking for people who love Him and are willing to be used by Him. You mean the world to Him; He loves you so much that He was willing to die that your life might have purpose.

If you are searching for something to fill the hole inside your heart, your search will end with Him. If you are looking for acceptance, He is the One who accepts you just as you are. If you are looking to be loved, He loves you more than you can ever imagine.

Before you move on, make sure your life is secure in His hands. Jesus is waiting for you to come to Him, whether you've walked away from Him over the years or if you've never known Him.

Do not put this book down before dedicating your life to Him.

Salvation Prayer

Dear Jesus,

I ask you to forgive me of my sins and to come into my heart. I turn my back on the way I've been living and allow you to change me. Thank you for dying on the cross for my sins and for loving me. Amen

<u>Speaking & Contact Information</u>

Columbine: Tragedy to Triumph

Lynn Shotwell
(303) 618-1779
Fax (303) 932-0378
Email: CTT Littleton@aol.com